REACHABLE

REACHABLE

HOW INDIGENOUS MISSIONARIES ARE CHANGING THE FACE OF MISSIONS

Jack Nelson

Worldlink International Ministries
Valley Forge, PA

Reachable:
How Indigenous Missionaries Are Changing the Face of Missions

Jack Nelson
Worldlink International Ministries
Valley Forge, PA

© 2016 by Worldlink International Ministries
All rights reserved

Worldlink International Ministries
PO Box 80202, Valley Forge, PA, 19484, USA
www.worldlinkonline.org

Cover design by Josh McGuire
Cover photo by Benjamin Palmer

ISBN 978-0-9982646-0-8

First printing 2016.

Printed in India

To Nancy: my wife, my partner in life, and my coworker in ministry. When you were five you said "yes" to Jesus. I'm not certain that you knew all that meant, but you have walked with and loved him since that day. Fifteen years later, you said "I do" to me. I am absolutely certain you had no idea what that would mean, but you have walked with me and loved me every day since then. Because of your encouragement, patience, and willingness to step into the unknown by faith, our lives, our ministry, and this book have all been possible.

To Michael (who I call Mitch): my brother, my inseparable boyhood friend, my sometimes tormentor, and the one whom God used to introduce me to my eternally-inseparable friend Jesus. You prodded me to understand and accept his grace gift of eternal life. Without starting there, we would never have gotten here.

To Jim and Bev: my mentors in my spiritual infancy who believed that a long-haired goofball athlete could, if submitted to Jesus, have potential to make a difference. You modeled Christ's love and passion and you kept any doubts about me quiet enough that I actually believed that God might want to use me to change the world.

Contents

Part Two: We Are Worldlink

Preface
A Tale of Two Strategies

God has commissioned this generation of believers to bring his love and Good News to this generation of lost and hurting people.

So what's the best way to reach the unreached masses of lost and hurting people around the world whom God has commissioned us to reach? For years, I thought the only way was to go as a Western missionary. Over 30 years ago, my wife, Nancy, and I decided to do just that. But God never opened that door. Then, over the years, I met indigenous Christians all over the world who were fulfilling the mission in their own countries and doing the same work I would have done as a Western missionary.

I compared these indigenous missionaries to me and considered two strategies for reaching others with the Good News.

- They already knew their language perfectly, but I would need years to learn it and a lifetime to master it.

- They were cultural insiders, while I would always be an outsider in my thinking and in the view of the local people.

- They were ready to serve immediately, whereas it would take me years to decide where to go, learn the language, raise funds, move my family, and be set to do the work.

- They would stay on mission for a lifetime, while my ministry would probably end in 10 or 20 years.

- They had ministry continuity, but I would have planned to return to the US every few years for visits, fundraising, education, and rest.

- They lived simply on the level of their peers, while even if I drastically lowered my American standard of living it would still be drastically higher than those I would serve.

- They could live on a few dollars a day, whereas the cost to send me and my family as Western missionaries would average hundreds of dollars a day.

I knew that there would always be some reason for Westerners to relocate, but as I saw these highly qualified, deeply passionate, and clearly called indigenous missionaries, God began to clarify a new mission strategy in my heart.

So, understanding God's commission to share his love and Good News with the world, and seeing the unique qualifications and advantages of indigenous missionaries in their own countries, I began to see something over and over.

I saw amazing opportunities for my indigenous missionary brothers and sisters, but I saw them struggling for resources (a $30/month salary, a bike, a few books to study or pamphlets to hand out...). Then I came back to the US and saw vast resources in the hands of my Christian brothers and sisters, but they had no opportunity or calling to relocate to the least-reached areas of the world.

Simply put, I saw **opportunities without resources** and **resources without opportunities**. And I did a dangerous thing. I told God, "You've got to do something about that!" **He did.** He led us to start Worldlink, to link indigenous missionaries with the resources they need to fulfill God's Great Commission and bring his love and Good News to lost and hurting people in their own lands.

This book contains some of the hundreds of remarkable stories of the lives and ministries of some of Worldlink's remarkable indigenous missionary partners. In addition, it explains some of the biblical reasons why every Christian should be involved in God's great mission of reaching those who are yet unreached with his Good News. Lastly, it lays out some of the basic philosophical and organizational foundations upon which we have built Worldlink.

It is amazing to see what God can do with a few hundred front-line indigenous missionaries in 32 countries throughout Asia, Africa, and Latin America. Every day, God is bearing fruit through the humble and faithful ministries of your indigenous brothers and sisters who are missionaries in their own countries.

My prayer is that these pages will do three things. First, I want to inform your head, so that you understand that you, little you, can make a big difference in partnership with an indigenous missionary in a remote part of the world. Secondly, I want to enflame your heart so that you have a passion to do your unique part to change a bit of our world. Finally, I want to inspire your hands to action.

Do you remember when you thought you could change the world? You were right!

Acknowledgments

I have heard it quipped at numerous times and by numerous people that, "If you find a turtle on a fencepost you know he had help getting there." I am that turtle.

This book could not have been written without the help of many people. Foremost, the remarkable indigenous missionary men and women whose stories I have the privilege of telling, along with the many hundreds more whose accounts and life stories this book cannot contain. Also, the past and current board, staff, donors, and volunteers of Worldlink International Ministries, whose loving sacrifices make possible the ministry of hundreds of indigenous missionaries around the world who are proving that even the most unlikely are reachable. You are too numerous to name here, yet your names are known and appreciated both by this turtle and by God, who will reward you greatly.

Introduction
The Midnight Advocate

The tapping on the darkened door was light, almost apologetic. It was clearly designed to arouse the sleeping homeowner but equally intended to do little to interfere with his family huddled and slumbering around him in the dark Israeli night.

Who could this be? This disturbance at this time of night was not only unexpected but borderline unacceptable.

Now, fully awakened by this intrusion, the man gently crept from under the blanket that sheltered him, along with his wife and their children. He cursed the frigid air and began gingerly navigating the way to the front door of his one-room home. Progressing through the darkness as much by memory as by sight, the cold touch of the hard dirt floor on his feet shocked his senses as much as this nighttime imposition shocked his sensibilities.

Surely this intruder must have an emergency. Surely he must know that opening the door at this time of night involves noisily removing the long locking poles and that will awaken the sleeping family. Surely, if this intrusion were not critically important, this man on the outside of the door would get a piece of the homeowner's mind that he could ill-afford to lose.

The second light tapping greeted his silence. "Who is it?" he whispered, inquiring.

"Ellazar? It's me, Amasa." The intruder whispered back. "I need your help.

"I am so sorry to bother you this late. I was sleeping just like you and I heard a knock on my door just like you. A dear friend of mine whom I have known and trusted for years has been on a long journey, a mission to get to a distant city for an important task. He stopped by my home and he hasn't eaten for days and needs food. He has walked long through the heat of many days and the cold of many nights and he has many more miles to go until his mission is accomplished.

"Ellazar, my friend needs food to sustain him now and propel him on his trip tomorrow. But I have nothing to give him. My cupboards are empty.

"Can you please give me some bread to meet this need? Can you please be a part of my friend's support?"

This is the beginning of the parable that Jesus tells in Luke 11. At least, in my retelling. If you know the passage, then you know that there were no names mentioned for the characters involved. I added them along with some speculative detail. Ellazar means "God Has Helped" and Amasa means "Burden." You probably can see why I chose those names.

Parenthetically, you know what a parable is, right? It is two male cows! A pair-a-bull.

Now, if you chuckled at that, my wife would say, "Don't laugh, it just encourages him." If you groaned at that, she would say, "See what I have to live with? Pray for me."

Actually, the word parable is a combination of two Greek words: *para* and *ballo*. Para means "next to," like a paramedic works next to a doctor, or a paralegal works next to a lawyer, or two parallel lines run next to each other. Ballo means to cast, to place, to set, or to hold.

So a parable in the Bible is a story in which a spiritual truth to be illustrated is thrown, placed, set, or held next to an earthly story that would be easily understood by the hearers.

Jesus explained the purpose for his parables in response to a direct question in Matthew 13:10ff. Basically, it was to make complicated truths easy to understand for those whose hearts were receptive. But of those with calloused hearts he says: "Though seeing, they do not see; though hearing, they do not hear or understand."

So, back to our parable. What, as Paul Harvey would ask, is "the rest of the story"?

The man in the house, even after hearing of the need, was reluctant to act. To meet the need expressed would be inconvenient to him and his family. It would cost him something. It would require a sacrifice. And, even though he had, in his possession, the resources to meet the need, he tells his desperate friend, "I can't get up and give you anything."

Jesus then comments on the man's hesitation: "I tell you, even though he will not get up and give you the bread because of friendship, yet because of your shameless audacity he will surely get up and give you as much as you need" (Luke 11:8).

Was it true that the sleeping homeowner could not meet the need? No! The fact that ultimately he gave as much as was needed proves that he had what was required.

So, what held the man back from meeting a life-saving, urgent, and known need? Jesus does not tell us so we don't know for certain. Perhaps he leaves it up to us to speculate.

Could he have been so comfortable in his warm bed that he simply did not want to give up his physical comfort or that of his family? Could he have feared that if he gave away his bread tonight that he or his family might not have bread enough for tomorrow? Could he have arrogantly reasoned that this traveler should have prepared for a journey this long and since he didn't he deserves to suffer the consequences?

We don't know the reason he hesitated, but we do know the reason he ultimately acquiesced to his neighbor's request and gave the needed provision. It was because his neighbor was humble enough and bold enough and persistent enough to ask until he got what he needed to meet the needs of his hurting and helpless friend.

Wow! Can you imagine what our culture might think of someone so daring, so intrepid as to keep asking until he gets the help he requires to meet another's need?

I can. I really can.

Before we talk about that, let me acknowledge that Jesus tells his parable to specific people in a specific context for a specific reason. Here, it is in the context of teaching on prayer and I believe it is to draw a contrast between the resistant homeowner, who hesitates to meet a need, and our receptive God, who is enthusiastic to hear our pleas and who promises: "Ask and it will be given to you; seek and you will find; knock and the door will be opened to you" (Luke 11:9).

In essence Jesus is saying, "In the first-century Jewish context it would be unthinkable for a man to turn aside a friend with a need when it was within the power of the man to meet the need, no matter how inconvenient. And if the friend can muster the boldness to come and ask he would be granted what he needed. Your God is not like the reluctant giver! He delights to give when you ask. So, get bold and get up and get over to his house and knock on the door and ask!"

But, besides encouraging you to pray boldly for my friends, whom you will meet in the following chapters of this book, why do I tell you this particular parable?

I share this parable because I think that you are more like our generous God than the hesitant homeowner, and I want to boldly knock on your door.

My friends, hundreds of indigenous missionaries on their mission's journey have a desperate need for help to sustain them today and supply them as they serve. In this book you will meet some of them. I will tell you their stories in detail as best I can (some names and details have been changed and locations omitted for security reasons). You will see their journey. You will see their character. You will see their commitment. You will see their calling. You will see what they could do if they had a little provision of bread to sustain them.

I have already seen these things. Worldlink can link those who have resources with those who need resources and who have opportunities to serve.

So I knock on your door as a midnight advocate. I ask, not for my needs, but for those of our current indigenous missionary partners and the needs of the hundreds, perhaps thousands more who wait to reach their own people with the love of God and the Good News of Jesus Christ.

I knock. And if you are moved to help, please open the door and share some of your bread.

At any time while reading this book you can grab the response card and mail it back, or go to our website at www. worldlinkonline.org, or call our team and sponsor one of God's choice servants like the ones you will meet in this book.

With your help linked to their work the unreached are *reachable*.

Part One
We Are Indigenous Missionaries

Undying Devotion:
Bobita's Story

Bobita lay bleeding and fading into unconsciousness on the dirt in front of the temple.

Beaten with bamboo rods by the enraged crowd of her own neighbors, relatives, and former friends she struggled to hold on. As the pain gave way to darkness she mouthed a silent prayer.

She did not want the beating she endured. She would do almost anything to stop it. But she knew that the one thing that would halt the savagery was the one thing she was unwilling to do. The words that held the keys to her release were not in her heart and would never, she vowed, cross her lips.

So, she steeled herself to the possibilities and committed her body to the One who had already saved her soul. And the darkness came.

The path that brought Bobita to that dusty field began a few years earlier. Bobita and Ramen were a typical village tribal couple. They lived with their tribal neighbors in a small home that was more of a shack by some standards. They were working as hard as they could. Because he had contracted tuberculosis, Ramen's lungs were weak and he could not do heavy physical labor. So he ran a small roadside store in a wooden shack that sold snacks to children and a few other items they could gather to sell. Bobita helped cook in a local school. They got by on their meager and sporadic salary.

They were, as all in their tribe were, Hindus. She was a temple helper and leader of the woman's group. While everything looked normal to their neighbors, they hid a tormenting secret in their home.

It started small and only happened occasionally. Then, over time, the seizures grew in both frequency and size. They were hard to trace but one thing seemed common: they happened whenever Bobita prayed to her Hindu gods or visited the village temple.

Fear would overcome her emotions, the darkness would enclose her vision, and tremors would overtake her body.

She dreaded going to the temple but believed that the idols there were the only answer to her problems, so she pushed on. But nothing offered relief.

She prayed with ultimate fervency to the gods of wood and stone but nothing helped. She gave offerings of flowers and food and money to placate whatever gods might be angry with her. But it did not help. She performed the rituals recommended by the priest. But nothing helped.

Losing hope, Bobita and Ramen went to the priest to see if there was any other god to whom they can pray or offering that they could make. The priest, who had already collected so much from them, had one last suggestion. He suggested a ritual at their home including many people visiting and offerings made for cleansing and then the kicker: a large cash gift given to the priest to appease the gods and make their trouble go away.

They had no more offerings, they had no more foods, they had no more gifts, and they had no more help. They retreated to their small shack and wondered about the future.

4

They resigned themselves to their fate. They knew that they would suffer and nothing could be done. They braced themselves for a lifetime of hopelessness with the faint dream that they might receive an upgrade when reincarnated.

But soon they would be introduced to hope they could not have imagined.

Each year, a large group of churches in that region, many planted by or led by Worldlink indigenous missionary partners, gather for a conference. They wait for the dry season and set up a temporary fabric building on an arid rice paddy. There, for four days, 1,000 to 1,500 Christians gather to celebrate what Jesus Christ has done for them. He took them from death to life. He took them from darkness to light. He brought them from helplessness and hopelessness to help for today and hope for eternity.

The location of the conference rotates around the district and is hosted by Christians in one of the villages. The groups from other villages set up tarps to live under for the four days and the large fabric building to house the meetings. A generator is brought in to create electricity for lights for the nighttime meetings and to power the amplification equipment.

And, boy, do they use the amplifier.

The teaching is made loud enough, not just for 1,500 people sitting on the ground shoulder to shoulder, but importantly to pump the messages into the surrounding village so that the villagers, who have precious little else to do in the dark and quiet night, can hear the Good News of Jesus Christ.

All day long local and guest preachers and teachers share God's Word and messages of encouragement for the gathered

Christians. When night falls the emphasis turns outward. Each evening the message centers on the great love of God and the amazing Gospel of Jesus Christ. The volume is cranked up so that the villagers can hear. Many from the surrounding villages gather outside of the fabric building and listen. Some would venture inside to find a place on the ground to sit and see the people who were sharing what, to the visitors, was such a strange message.

That year, the conference came to a village close to Ramen and Bobita. In the quiet of the dark at night, Ramen heard the distant sound of men's voices over the loudspeaker. He could not make out what they were saying, but the crowd's singing sounded joyous in the midst of his desperation. The teaching sounded upbeat to his downtrodden heart. And so he ventured into the darkness.

Ramen walked the short couple of miles on the moon-lit dirt roads between his village and the conference site. The air was cool and moist at that time of year, but there was no danger of rain. He was wrapped in his only coat but still walked as briskly as his weak lungs would let him to keep his skinny frame warm.

He followed the sound until he arrived at the conference site. He joined the crowd of curious onlookers outside the tent and listened to news that shocked his senses.

The teachers spoke of a God who was not one of thousands of gods, but the only true God. They spoke of a God who was not vengeful, but was loving. They spoke of a love that was demonstrated by God paying a price of blood for Ramen's wrongdoings, which he knew were many. They spoke of a God who cared about the suffering of people and would listen to their pleas. And they spoke of a God who was powerful enough to answer their petitions for their good and his glory.

Deep into the night when the meetings ended, Ramen sought out the leaders of the conference. "It sounds like your God can help people in need. Can he help my wife?" he probed.

"We know he *can*! We don't know if he *will*. But why don't we ask." They followed Ramen back to his home and met Bobita. They heard her story and crushed heart. When the men shared Jesus'Good News with Ramen and Bobita, the couple responded in faith and trusted Christ as their Savior. The leaders surrounded them and fervently prayed that God would release Bobita from her suffering.

That was the last time they would ever need to pray that prayer because she never again had seizures.

Nine months after that evening, I met Bobita. I had come to meet with indigenous missionaries and to teach in a nearby town. She came at the invitation of the church leaders.

During those previous nine months, she had been guarded in sharing about what God has done in her life. She knew that people from their tribe who left the temple were taking a large risk. But she knew what Christ has done for her and was growing in her knowledge and faith and wanted to step up for the God who stepped down into humanity to save her.

Three weeks later she did step up. She and Ramen and five other believers from their village publicly declared their faith in Jesus Christ through baptism in a murky drainage pond.

And then the persecution began.

In many Hindu areas, believing in Jesus is not really a problem. Many think it is nice to add another God to the thousands or perhaps millions that you acknowledge and worship. It is when an individual declares the exclusivity of Christ that the trouble begins.

These new believers were saying in essence, "We know that there is only one true God. All the idols that we have followed are wood and stone and metal at best and demonic at worst. The true God created the world, and people rebelled against him. We, too, have gone away from him, but now we are turning back and accepting Jesus as the only true savior."

To many Westerners, with a very individualistic culture and religious experience, it seems a strange thing to persecute people who "leave the faith." But, in this South Asian tribal culture, the individual is part of the community. And when an individual turns their back on the village gods, the neighbors don't think that the gods will only be mad at the individual, they believe that the gods will be mad at the community for allowing part of their tribe to turn their back on the gods. Therefore, they reason, the Snake God will let the snakes bite our children and the Water God will dry up the well and we will have no water, and the Rain God will withhold the rain in his anger.

The neighbors in their village and their tribesmen from other villages feared the worst. And therefore, the neighbors will do anything necessary to restore those who depart back to worshiping the gods of the past. And that's what they did to Bobita and Ramen.

It started off mild, with pleading. When that did not work it moved to arguing. When that did not work it moved to yelling and taunting. No results there led to Bobita and Ramen being declared unclean. This meant that nobody would go to Ramen's small store and so he had to close it down. That meant that no parent would let their child eat food prepared by Bobita at the school and so she was fired. Guards were stationed around their home to watch and warn any visitors that they should not enter or they risked being unclean.

When that did not lead Bobita and Ramen to recant, the neighbor's fear turned to fury. The village elders, the temple priests, and about 80 neighbors gathered together. They seized Bobita and Ramen and one other new believer. They dragged them to the field in front of the temple.

The three young Christians would not deny Jesus.

They were forced to sign papers giving their home away to relatives and yet they would not recant. The neighbors mocked communion by saying that Christians drink blood and then forced Bobita and Ramen to drink urine and yet they would not recant.

When all of this failed to get these three courageous believers to turn their back on their Savior, the fear that had become fury then became force.

A group of the young men in the crowd gathered bamboo sticks and logs and began beating the believers. It was not until Bobita sank into unconsciousness that the savagery stopped. The three bodies were left. Perhaps this would teach them their lesson.

They learned a lesson, but not the one their tormentors wished.

The Christians who had lead them to Christ heard about the beatings and came to help. They took Bobita to a distant hospital and paid for her care. One woman, who would later become Bobita's closest friend, would not leave her side for the days that she spent in the hospital.

The Christians housed the beaten believers in their own homes for many weeks and nursed them back to health. On the other side of the world, Christians were doing their part to help. Alerted by Worldlink, they were praying fervently for these brothers and sisters they would never meet.

Slowly, the healing came to their bodies as the courage had come to their souls. The local Christians urged Ramen and Bobita to move from their village to live with the Christians in a village that would be safer. But Ramen and Bobita would hear nothing of that. They moved back into their own home.

About 10 weeks after their beatings and a couple of weeks after they moved back into the village where they were beaten, I met with Ramen and Bobita again at the annual conference where they had come to faith the year before.

I asked them why they did not turn back and deny Christ. Bobita said that she could never do that after all Jesus has done for her.

I asked them directly, believing that I already knew the answer, why they would move back into the village where they were so traumatized and so terrorized. They looked at each other and then looked at me and said, "If we don't go back and live there, who will tell them about Jesus?"

For an hour we sat together and shared in their story. I was humbled and amazed and convicted. They were joyous in their faith and committed to our Savior. But they did have one deep pain that remained.

Because they had become Christians, their daughter was taken away from them. In their culture, the oldest male relative has power over the clan. In this case, Bobita's brother decided that, since she was unclean and unfit, their teenage daughter needed to go live with him.

10

We wept together over this heartbreak and prayed that God would protect their daughter and reunite them in his timing.

God's timing is not always our timing. The months went on and their daughter was not returned. Although many good things were happening.

Bobita was given a job cooking and helping at a Children's Home that Worldlink supports nearby. The local believers bought them a cow and some chickens so they would have milk and eggs. Many in their tribe grew weary of persecuting them and so the guards were no longer at their house. Some neighbor women, having seen Bobita before and after her conversion and witnessing the depth of her faith, began visiting her and asking her about her new God. Many became secret believers.

But their greatest heartache still persisted. Their daughter was estranged from them. They had to sneak short visits with her on her way to or from school. Her uncle, in whose home she lived, would not allow her to visit the church that her parents attended in a neighboring village. The weeks dragged into months and the months into a year.

And then it was conference time again.

By God's grace, I returned again that next year for the big area conference. I never tire of watching the joyous singing and celebration of humble brothers and sisters in distant lands. I never tire of teaching and encouraging faith-filled believers who soak up God's Word like a sponge. And they, it seems to me, do not tire as they will sit crossed-leg on the straw-covered dirt floor for hour after hour to listen to the truth from God's Word.

11

When the last night of the conference came we had the opportunity to, once again, share the simple Good News of Jesus Christ: there is a God who created and loves you. You and I and every human being have walked away from him by thoughts, words, and deeds. The Bible calls those sins. Because God is just, our sins must be punished. God so loved you that he took the punishment that you deserved and, in the person of Jesus Christ, died for your sins on the cross. Because of Jesus' payment, God offers you full and free forgiveness, reconciliation to him, a meaningful life now, and an eternity in his presence. All you have to do to receive those unimaginable blessings is to believe that he did this for you and receive his free gift by faith.

At the end of the meeting, we gave the opportunity for anyone who had made that faith decision, whether in the fabric building or listening outside, to come forward and be counseled on how to live this new life they had just received.

As I scanned the faces of the 30 or so people who came to the front of the crowd, my eyes widened and then filled with tears. There with a smile as wide as her face was Bobita walking arm in arm with her daughter.

Her daughter snuck out of her uncle's home to be at the meeting. She had heard from her mother about this amazing God. She had witnessed the life change that had gone on in their family and others who became Christians. She could no longer deny that Jesus was real and could change lives and eternities. So there she was making her own commitment to Jesus.

Bobita's undying commitment to Jesus Christ has now resulted in not only many villagers coming to know Jesus, but also the one villager she cared the most about—her daughter—coming to Jesus.

Bobita now serves Jesus as an indigenous missionary. She shares her story and the truth of the Good News that changed her life with anyone who will listen. And many, who are as hopeless as she was, are listening. Bobita looks back and remembers the time that she had the chance to make the beating stop. She said "no" to the temptation to deny Christ then, and many are saying "yes" to the opportunity to accept Christ now. She told me it was worth it.

For pictures of Bobita and more information about Worldlink, please go to www.worldlinkonlinc.org.

So Much with So Little: John's Story

It was one of those moments that I believe I will never forget and one which God used to change the trajectory of my life. I sat across from John in a small office and listened to his story and the story of his ministry. I was gripped with crushing horror then by uplifting anticipation and finally by inspired resolve.

John is from Liberia, West Africa. I had known him for several years because of the ministry he led which brought help and healing to children and youth in that then-dreadful war-torn country. John was born there. He lived through the hell-on-earth of war there. He served his Lord there in horrible conditions that would have made any North American I know run to the airport and fly home. But John could not fly home to some safe place because he was home and he was not going anywhere else.

Liberia's history is unknown to most North Americans and is obscure to the rest (except for a few academics, some NGOs, a bunch of interested Christians, and the estimated few hundred thousand people in United States with Liberian backgrounds). Some knowledge is important to understand John's story.

Although people from the north and east of Africa had migrated into the area that is now Liberia for centuries and European powers had established trading posts there, it wasn't until the 1800s that Liberia became formalized as a country.

In the early 1800s, groups were formed to help return freed American slaves to Africa. While the motivation of individuals and groups associated with this movement varied greatly, some noble and some quite sinister, the results were that, over the ensuing decades, growing numbers of freed blacks were helped to relocate to Africa. Many from the United States and the Caribbean were relocated to the area that is now Liberia.

In 1847, Liberia declared its independence. The name of Liberia was chosen because the returning slaves had their liberty. The capital, Monrovia, was named after the fifth US President, James Monroe.

For many reasons, most notably their higher education and ability to relate to colonial powers, the former slaves and their families held the economic and political power in Liberia, even though they were only a very small percentage of the country's population. Although its history was dotted by unrest, occasional coups, and violent changes of power, for the most part, long-simmering tribal, economic, and political tensions were held in check in Liberia until the 1980s. It was then that Civil War engulfed the country.

Liberia's Civil Wars, like many African conflicts, included the brutal practice of the kidnapping and use of child soldiers. A warlord's militia would drive into a village. They would round up the children at gunpoint and take them back to their camp. They would manipulate, threaten, drug, and train the boys into killing machines. The girls were used as sex slaves to reward the boys and men in the militia.

It was that unimaginable evil of child abuse that formed the foundation of my first meeting with John.

When John and I sat in that little office, the war had begun to settle down. Many of the militias were releasing their child soldiers and concubines. They reasoned, "You're not fighting for me any longer and I don't want to have to pay for your food, so go home."

And so thousands of these children were making their way either to their former villages or into the city of Monrovia. And just as the seemingly impotent government was struggling, their families and the churches were struggling to cope with that influx. With hearts of compassion and love they wanted to help these children who had been so brutalized, but they had no training or experience. They were asking, "What do we do with a 12-year-old boy who has been killing people for five years? What do we do with a 15-year-old girl who has been serially sexually abused for the last five years?"

John's ministry to children and youth was not big and it was not perfect, but it was poised to do significant work in the lives of some of these desperately needy children. As John related the circumstances in Liberia, both he and I knew that he and his small team had a tremendous opportunity in place before them to change the lives and the eternities of children, youth, and their families. I was excited to anticipate what God might do.

I asked John how they were responding to this new opportunity. He lowered his head, shook it slightly, and said, "We can't. We have no money to pay our field staff. I have had to release most of my team to find other jobs if they can or to grow a few crops to feed their families. The economy is in shambles and even the civil servants have not been paid in almost a year. So, I don't know that we can respond."

I can be a reasonably brash North American, so I just asked John upfront, "How much do you pay your field staff?"

"We pay them $35 US a month," he replied.

I was shocked! My first reaction was, "Can you repeat that?" John speaks with a heavy West African accent (he says that I am the one with an accent). Perhaps I misunderstood. Surely, it can't be that inexpensive.

John repeated, "We pay them $35 US a month."

It was one of those moments where God takes a post-it-note and jams it on your heart and says, "Remember this!" Not only do I remember it, but it has transformed my thinking and my planning.

Because my wife, Nancy, and I had planned to go to another country as North American missionaries, we knew what the cost of sending us to other countries to do missionary work could be. Depending on where we wanted to go, where we wanted to live, and what percentage our sending agency would take, it would require somewhere between $30,000 and $70,000 a year to send and keep our family in another country.

For the first time it really hit me. I was considering raising and using that much money to empower one missionary to reach people for Christ when the same amount of money could pay for 165 of John's local Liberian missionary partners.

I had to sit long and think hard to answer the question of whether I think I am 165 times more effective at reaching Liberians than a Liberian.

Now, let me take a quick parenthesis because I know that some who are reading this are thinking I am saying something that I am not. For some, the immediate reaction might be defensiveness, which can obscure communication. I am not saying that hundreds of years of sending missionaries from one country to another was inappropriate or ineffective. Clearly, that strategy has been used by God to bring the Good News of Jesus Christ and help and hope to people around the world. But just because something worked in the past does not mean it is the best strategy for the present or the future. That decision must be made on other criteria.

Just because I argue that there may be a new and more effective way of doing something does not insult or degrade the value of something else. Let me see if I can illustrate that with a reference to transportation. If I were to say that a Boeing 777 Dreamliner or an Airbus 380 is a marvelous and efficient way to get from the United States to the United Kingdom, would anybody think that I was insulting ocean liners? I don't think so. So, by arguing that a traveler just may get to their destination faster and cheaper on a plane than on a ship, I'm not saying that ships did not do the Yeoman's work of transportation in the past or that they do not have a place in modern transportation today.

In the same way, challenging concerned Christians to rethink the way we have thought about Great Commission ministry around the world—and its relationship to our responsibility to wisely steward God's resources entrusted to us—does not mean that the sacrificial, godly, and impacting ministry of Western missionaries in the past was not valuable. In fact, their work set the stage for what can be done by front line indigenous missionaries like John's team in Liberia today.

18

Western missionary activity has an essential place in reaching the world for Jesus. There are some places where there is no local option and some activities that simply cannot be done by local or national workers yet. Medical teams need to go to places where there are no doctors. People with technical linguistic ability need to go to places where local languages must be reduced to writing and the Bible translated into those languages.

I believe that there will always be a place for servant-minded cross-cultural ministry. I do have some very strong convictions on how foreigners should live in other countries and who should be calling the shots, but that does not preclude a place in God's plan for Westerners relocating to other lands.

When thinking of international ministry, however, we must admit that most frontline evangelistic outreach/church planting ministry and most mercy ministries that care for the physical and emotional needs of hurting people can be done much more efficiently by people who are making $35, $100, or $250 a month rather than someone who needs $3,000, $4,000, or $6,000 of God's money every month.

There are a lot of factors that must be inputted into any equation determining ministry efficiency. We are only talking about my shock at the difference of cost here. So, let's put aside the arguments of whether a Liberian can reach Liberians better than I can; whether Pakistanis have access to people whom I cannot reach; whether Indians understand Indian culture more clearly than I do; whether readiness or longevity or continuity have any place in the equation.

Let's make a crazy leap and claim that I am 10 times as effective as John in reaching Liberians. Even assuming that, would it make sense for me to send one Jack or 165 Johns? Even if John's team make 10 times more than they did on that day in the office, we would still have 16.5 of them doing the work for the cost of one of me and my family.

Again, I am not saying that we should not decide that a Westerner is called to go to another land, but I am saying that before we decide to invest the price of sending a Westerner, good stewardship demands that we ask if we can confidently say that they are doing more than 10 or 165 indigenous Christian missionaries like John and his team. Indigenous missionaries can do so much with so little that it makes no sense to ignore their calling and our opportunity to partner with them.

Since that meeting with John, I have been back and forth to Liberia several times and have seen the team in action. God used that simple discussion, and the post-it-note stuck on my heart, to plant the seed that he nurtured to grow into Worldlink International Ministries. We have, and are, supporting John's team and others who are reaching the unreached in Liberia and 31 other countries for Jesus at the time I write this.

Our indigenous missionary partners are doing so much, for so many, with so little. I will never forget it.

For pictures of John and more information about Worldlink, please go to www.worldlinkonline.org.

A Greater Plan:
Barnabas's Story

Four times each year I receive reports of the life and ministry of each of Worldlink's indigenous missionary partners. The reports outline how they and their family are doing, what ministry activities they have done and plan to do, and what results God has brought about.

When I received Barnabas's report I saw something I had never seen before that time.

Some years earlier, Barnabas had gone out to the forested villages of India to share the Gospel of Christ with a passion and burden to reach people whom he knew had never heard about Jesus. When he decided to work in theses remote villages, he built a little hut for himself and his family to live in. It was constructed, in typical fashion, out of mud and thatch. This dwelling acted as his home and his ministry center and it served him well for quite a while.

As I read his report, and that of the Area Leader, Suku, they both asked for prayer because Barnabas's house had fallen down. This is not normal, so I wrote to Suku for details.

In their part of India, the rains start in June and do not stop until September. When the rains are gentle, it waters the rice paddies and fills the rivers. But when the toughest storms come it devastates the very poor population.

The monsoon rains had just come, and Barnabas's house was demolished. Suku sent me a picture of himself and another Worldlink partner standing with Barnabas on the rubble of his shattered home. Barnabas stood in the middle with his shoulders slumped. His two ministry partners stood on either side of him with a hand on each shoulder, while they prayed for him.

What might have been going through Barnabas's mind? "God, why would you let this happen? How could this be for your glory and my good? What do you want me to do? I thought that you had sent me here to serve you. You know I have no money to rebuild my house. My dream is shattered."

As he stood on the rubble of what was his home, he looked confused and heartbroken. Humanly speaking it looked like God was not concerned, as though even if God did notice Barnabas, he was too busy to help and Barnabas was forgotten.

Have you ever felt that way? If so, then you understand how Barnabas felt. And you understand the feelings of two biblical characters whom we meet in Luke 24.

These first followers of Christ felt like their world had fallen apart. They had come to the end of their hopes and dreams. Recorded for us is a glimpse of them.

We read in Luke 24:13-14: "Now that same day two of them were going to a village called Emmaus, about seven miles from Jerusalem. They were talking with each other about everything that had happened."

We know from the Scriptures that a week earlier Jesus had walked those same dusty roads and made his way into Jerusalem.

He came in on what we now call Palm Sunday and the masses cheered as he rode in on a donkey, fulfilling Zechariah 9:9 which says, "Your king will ride in on the foal of a donkey." They shouted, "Hosanna! Hosanna!" which means save, savior, you are the one! "Blessed is he who comes in the name of the Lord!" they shouted, echoing Psalm 118.

Basically they were saying, "You are the Messiah who will save us from these despicable Romans who are oppressing us." They thought they knew God's plan. "You will set up your kingdom and Israel will be raised up to a place of prominence. It's going to be great! We figured it out!"

But there was only one problem with their thinking: that wasn't God's plan.

Isaiah 55:8-9 says: "'For my thoughts are not your thoughts, neither are your ways my ways,' declares the LORD. 'As the heavens are higher than the earth, so are my ways higher than your ways and my thoughts than your thoughts.'" They had assumed they had this Messiah thing figured out and it was all tied up in a nice little bow, but over a week's time their package started to unravel.

Instead of driving the hated oppressors out of the land, Jesus drives the ecclesiastical hucksters out of his Father's house. Instead of speaking truth to the powerful Romans and putting them down, he offends the sensitivities of the religious leaders and stirs them up. Instead of being driven by their praises to his rightful place on the throne of Israel, Jesus ends up being driven through the streets and up a hill to be crucified. The glorious

23

Savior, mocked ingloriously. Stripped, exposed, naked, killed. He began the week looking like a conquering king, invincible. And he ends the week looking like a common criminal. Dead on a cross, frail and failed. Rejected by his countrymen, rejected by those who followed him, and it looked, to human eyes, like God himself had rejected him.

And so now it is Sunday afternoon. These two followers are saying to themselves, "Passover is over and so are our hopes, so let's just go home." Their shoulders slumped as they walked along. As they slowly shuffled along the seven-mile trip to their home in Emmaus, they discussed the devastating events of the past week. Suddenly, Jesus himself came up and walked along their journey with them, but they were kept from recognizing him. And he asked them, "What are you discussing together as you walk along?" One of them asked him, "Are you the only one visiting Jerusalem who does not know the things that have happened there in these days?" They were incredulous that someone could have been in Jerusalem and not heard the news that engulfed the city. They might have thought, "Have you been living under a rock these past three days?" Well, he had, sort of.

"What things?" he asked.

"About Jesus of Nazareth," they replied. "He was a prophet, powerful in word and deed before God and all the people. The chief priests and our rulers handed him over to be sentenced to death, and they crucified him; but *we had hoped* that he was the one who was going to redeem Israel..."

Adding insult to injury now they continued, "What's more, it is the third day since all this took place. In addition, some of

24

our women amazed us. They went to the tomb early this morning but didn't find his body. They came and told us that they had seen a vision of angels, who said he was alive. Then some of our companions went to the tomb and found it just as the women had said, but they didn't see him there."

"We had hoped...." Three of the saddest words in Scripture. There they stood with shoulders slumped on the pile of their shattered dreams.

Today, we know the rest of the story. We know that Jesus didn't come to set up an earthly, political kingdom. We know that he came to set up an eternal kingdom of redeemed people who have heard the Good News, understood what God has offered to them, and, by faith, received salvation along with spiritual blessings beyond their wildest dreams. We see it all clearly now as his followers. We see that they were hoping in lesser things, but God had a greater plan. A plan so much better than they could comprehend.

That's the story of Cleopas and his friend. And that is Barnabas's story as well.

I looked at the picture of Barnabas again as he was standing on the rubble of what was his home. Then I emailed an inquiry to Suku, the missionary leader in the region. "Suku," I wrote, "how much would it cost to build Barnabas his home again?" He replied that it would cost about $200. Then he added, "But if we wanted to build it out of block, it would be about $1000, for a much sturdier house."

Through a series of events and a donor in the US, God provided $1,000, and the money was sent over for the new house to be built. With that amount they could build a building that was about 10 x 20 feet with two rooms and a corrugated roof. Because Barnabas is a simple village man who doesn't know project management, Suku was happy to oversee the project.

The plans were drawn and the rock and mortar foundation was laid by Barnabas and his family. The brick was purchased and brought out to the village. Then it was time to begin building.

In order to build, Suku needed to search for a bricklayer. Suku lived three hours away from the village. So, as he drove toward Barnabas's area, he came to a market area at a place where his road crossed a similarly sized road. In their culture, day laborers wait at the crossroads for someone to offer them work.

Suku stopped his little car, went up to the group of men and said, "I need someone who can travel out to a village and who is able to stay out there for about a week to lay brick for a small house. Can any of you do that?" Suku later told me that there was one young man who came forward to do the job. He said, "I can go. I can do that work. I have no family obligations."

So they negotiated the price and hopped into Suku's car. As they were driving along toward Barnabas's remote village, the young man asked what village they were going to. When Suku told him, the young man became strangely silent. He inquired further, "Whose house are we working on?" Suku told him, "Barnabas's house." At that the young man blurted out, "Please stop the car. I'm so sorry, but I can't go with you. I need to get out. I need to return to the market." Suku, realizing that this was not a normal reaction, began to question the young man about why he was so disturbed. Suku found out his name was Karthic. And, after a long discussion, he found that Karthic was Barnabas's son.

Years before this "chance" meeting, Karthic had made a fateful choice. He left the family when Barnabas had moved to that village. He had told his father that he had wanted nothing to do with this village life or his God. He went to the nearby city, learned the trade of brick-laying, and was making his living hustling jobs as best he could.

After Suku counseled with Karthic, he agreed to go back to the village. When they arrived at the village where his father, Barnabas, his mother, and two sisters lived as missionaries, there was an amazing reconciliation between father and son.

Over the course of the next week, there was also an amazing reconciliation between Karthic and God, his heavenly father, as this young man committed himself to faith in Jesus Christ for the forgiveness of his sins. He built the house and with it came the building of a new relationship with God. The house became a better ministry center than the one before. It was bigger and sturdier. As the house was dedicated to the Lord, the prayer was, "Lord, you have done great things and reconciled our family, now use this house to reconcile many to you."

And that is what is happening.

A short time later, I visited Barnabas in his new home with one room for his family and one for his ministry center. We rejoiced over what the Lord had done. We shared a vision of what the Lord would do in the future.

As I sat there in the remote village watching the joy of the family, I thought of that picture from months earlier—the one with Barnabas's slumped shoulders and broken dreams. At that moment, all he could have hoped for was another mud hut. He hoped for lesser things, but God had a greater plan.

I thought of how often I do the same. I envision and would settle for a small result, but God has a greater plan.

I sat off to the side of the small property and watched as Barnabas and his family, Suku and his family, and a few other partners who traveled with us celebrated in their mother language. I did not understand the words but I knew exactly how they felt. I chuckled to myself as I imagined a scenario. What if I went to Barnabas and asked him, "Barnabas, if I could turn back time to the day before your house fell down and I could guarantee that the rain would stop and the house would stand, would you like to go back and have your dreams, or would you take what God has done even with the troubles?" I think that I know his answer.

For pictures of Barnabas and more information about Worldlink, please go to www.worldlinkonline.org.

This Cannot Prevent Us from Doing the Work of the Lord: Francis's Story

I want to introduce you to a friend and colleague of mine. His name is Francis. He lives in the Central African Republic (CAR), a country in the Northern tier of sub-Saharan Africa. It is bordered by Sudan and South Sudan, the Democratic Republic of the Congo, and Congo, Cameroon, and Chad. Let me give you a little history so that you can understand current realities of the CAR.

The CAR was settled thousands of years ago by nomadic tribesmen who were pushed south by the desertification of the Sahara. They became an agrarian society and during the 16th to the 19th centuries tribes settled all throughout the area. Then from Egypt and other northern African areas, Muslim slave traders raided the area and took people away from this tribal area and sold them into North Africa, Arabia, and Europe.

When some of the local tribes saw how lucrative this practice was, they also began to raid each other's tribes. There was one tribe who became immensely successful at this immensely awful practice. The Bobangi saw an opportunity. They began taking captured members of other tribes down the Ubangi River to the Atlantic coast where they would be sold into slavery in the West Indies and the Americas. During this time the tribes were fighting against each other in increasingly difficult efforts to keep from being raided and traded. This intertribal animosity continued for centuries even up until and after the 1880s when the French (and other Europeans) came in to "colonize" the area.

Not until 1910 did the slave trade officially stop. While the French were ruling there was no official slavery, but life wasn't any great bargain for the people. The Europeans began to plant coffee and cotton and to mine the region's rich natural resources. They built railroads to transport all of these products to the coast for easy export.

All the while, the native people were treated terribly. One of the things the colonial power did was to separate the tribes and keep them warring against each other so that they wouldn't unite and overthrow the colonial powers. And that tribal animosity remained even after independence in the mid-1900s. A cycle of coup after coup would throw out the governments and install new ones.

Now, fast forward to today. You have massive intertribal animist, a corrupt government, a civil war with battles arising regularly, a broken economy, and a fractured populace who are forced to deal with all of this. They are compelled to take sides, take cover, or take off.

In this context enter Francis and Melvina. They are a young couple who had come to know Christ and wanted to share that incredible knowledge with their friends and neighbors. They became Worldlink partners about 10 years ago. And over that time they have seen thousands of people come to know Christ in the midst of this very dark and bleak situation. In very unplanned ways God has used them.

In one of Francis's very early Worldlink Partner Reports he shares: "We continue to proclaim the Good News of salvation in

Jesus Christ and in churches that invite us. On our way to Younde, one of our vehicles broke down in a village where we were stranded for five days." When I read this in Francis's report, I immediately thought of how inconvenient it is to serve in environments like his where a simple car problem can strand you for five days. I thought, "What a pain." But that's not how Francis reacted. Here is the next line from his report: "This gave us the opportunity to thoroughly evangelize the village. Thank God for about 30 people who received the Lord as their savior as a result of this ministry. Pray that the Lord may sustain them."

Shortly thereafter, Francis sent me a photo of himself and a young soldier named Placid. Placid was a non-religious man, but Francis told him about Jesus and gave him a Bible just before Placid went off to a far outpost as an army soldier. They lost contact until a couple of months later when Placid returned and he told Francis this story: "I was out at the outpost and we were raided by one of the militias. And all of the men in my company were killed except me as I escaped into the jungle. I believe that God allowed me to escape with my Bible so that I could tell others about the message, and I want to be a missionary like you are."

But success in ministry isn't without pain. In 2012, Francis and Melvina lived through a day of tragedy that none of us would ever want to experience. Esdras, their seven-year-old healthy son, woke up in the morning, became sick by late morning, and by afternoon was dead, likely of a disease that would be easily treatable in a more-developed country. Francis wrote, "This sudden departure is extremely difficult for us to comprehend, but we keep going because God knows everything. We continue to faithfully serve Him. We do not subscribe to the custom of the

CAR." (The traditional custom is for witch doctors to come and make sacrifices to the gods to stop evil spirits from preventing that soul from going into the afterlife.) "We instead buried him in the family cemetery in our village worshipping our God, surrounded by brothers and sisters in Christ." Francis sent me a picture of the funeral.

Francis and Melvina said that they would keep going, and that is exactly what they did. They continued to serve God faithfully. The ministry progressed and they continued to see fruit. The family continued, unified in love for the Lord and each other. Melvina became pregnant again, this time with twins. They were born healthy and brought joy to the family.

But, as usual, joy was mixed with difficulty. In October of 2013, the war erupted again and the battle around them raged. Still they continued to minister because they were compelled to. Francis wrote, "Thanks for your prayers. God has kept us so far despite the sad situation and rebellion. Activities in the capital not to mention those in the interior have ground to a halt. Loss of electricity and water. Almost all administrative buildings, hospitals, and private companies have been looted. We live daily with the sounds of gunfire and under pressure from more than 3,000 rebels in our town. The children, even our babies, are constantly frightened and sick. But all this cannot prevent us from doing the work of the Lord."

I continued to marvel at their response to trial after tragedy. A couple of more months went by and Francis and Melvina were driven out of their home by the rebels, and their family home was looted and burned to the ground. They resettled near the capital in an IDP (Internally Displaced Persons) Camp. It had been a school, but now 1,000 people, who like Francis and his family had been forced to abandon everything and run for their lives, had gathered and were living there in classrooms and under trees. For two years they continued to live there.

Now, what do you do when you want to continue doing the work of the Lord and you are a refugee living in a school with 1,000 other displaced people? You start Bible studies! You share with people the Good News about Jesus! You become the pastor of the refugee camp! And that's what Francis and Melvina have been doing for two years. They are bringing help and healing as counselors and pastors to the hurting around them.

In September 2015 the fighting again made its way to the capital nearby. Francis wrote, "I thank the Lord for his love toward me. Since September 26, 2015, when violence began in the capital where I live with my family, God has indeed shown his power. The destruction of life and religious and family properties and the sound of gunfire reduced only in the last few days. I acknowledge the hand of God through the prayers raised on my behalf and especially for my country. Please be reassured that our God and Father is answering your prayers. As you know we have been taking refuge in the campus. The crisis has increased the number of people taking refuge in this campus. We now have 2,578 people living with us. An NGO (Non-government Organization) donated a huge tent. By the grace of God, I continue to serve. We have started a prayer chain with displaced people and we meet every day from 5 to 6 o'clock in the afternoon for exhortation and prayer. We have already celebrated two Sunday worship meetings. I organize meetings in the eight tents and classrooms which house most of the people. Most refugees here are women and children. Most have no home because the militia have burned them, and hundreds of church buildings have been destroyed, including the one that housed our office. As for my family, my wife and five children and three orphans under our care are all fine. The children are recovering gradually after this very difficult time. God continues to strengthen me personally and I have joy in serving in this new field of ministry."

One of the amazing things that I have witnessed repeatedly in the lives and ministries of my indigenous missionary brothers and sisters is the fierce tenacity with which they fulfill their ministry calling coupled with a remarkable flexibility. Not only do they have access to lands where I cannot go, but they continue to minister in circumstances that would repel the heartiest Western missionaries I know.

Simply put, they go where we cannot go, and they stay when we would not stay. This was brought home to me vividly during the founding years of Worldlink's ministry. Shortly after we began in 2002, the US involvement with conflicts in Afghanistan and Iraq began to unfold. I went to a Christian Foundation to share our vision and ask for help. They listened intently and seemed genuinely supportive. In fact, they have regularly supported Worldlink since then. But when I asked for funding, the representative replied, "We would love to help but we have no funding available at this time because we have just given many emergency grants to get [Western] missionaries out of Afghanistan and surrounding countries."

That very week I had received an email from Ayub, an early indigenous missionary partner from a country that borders Afghanistan. He said that because the war was coming to Afghanistan, many Afghans were pouring into their country. So he had gathered as many blankets and provisions as he could and borrowed a truck. He and some co-ministers were going to drive to the border and meet the refugees, hoping that they would be more open to God's love in their desperate circumstances.

As I sat in the office of that foundation, I imagined Ayub and his rag-tag group of indigenous missionaries piled into a truck full of relief materials, chugging toward the border, praying for an opportunity to share God's love, while on the same road, the SUVs of Western agencies were heading in the opposite direction full of people praying for safe deliverance to their homes.

I'm not disparaging Westerners who leave for home amidst regional conflicts. I am just pointing out that when nationals "leave for home" they stay in the middle of the conflict zones because that *is* their home. And, like Francis and Ayub, they flex their ministry plans and serve where they are and in the face of difficulties. As Francis said, "But all this cannot prevent us from doing the work of the Lord."

For pictures of Francis and more information about Worldlink, please go to www.worldlinkonline.org.

To Whom Will They Listen?: Aiomi's Story

It was a swift kick in my attitudinal rear. And I deserved it. And it has served me well.

I sat on the hard wooden bench in the only seemingly stable structure in the center of a makeshift refugee squatters' camp on the island of Sri Lanka. To my right sat Ravi, a wonderful godly man whom I had known for some years because of his affiliation with the ministry with which I served and who was translating for me. In front of me sat about 75 women with small children of various ages. All of them bore one important thing in common with Aiomi, the woman who stood before them: they were all widows with small children, although they found themselves in that condition for different reasons.

A few hours before I sat in that refugee camp I sat with Aiomi, and she shared how she got to this point of ministry for Jesus.

Just years prior, Aiomi had seemed to have everything a young Sri Lankan Christian woman could want. She had a vibrant relationship with Jesus. She had a wonderful husband whom she had married and what she called a "love marriage." Most marriages in Sri Lanka are arranged by parents, but she and Clement had fallen in love and their parents allowed them to marry. And soon thereafter came a succession of three beautiful children.

Clement was a good and godly Christian man. He loved his family and loved to work hard for their future. Though he worked as a poor laborer, he had worked hard enough and saved long enough to start his own business. The business he was going to start involved buying a small three-wheeled taxi with which he could travel around town, serving people's transportation needs and retaining the profits for himself and his family.

The purchase of this vehicle and the promise that it represented was such a big event in their extended family that many family members gathered together on the evening that the vehicle was to be bought. They were going to celebrate as Clement became a business owner.

Early that morning Clement left on a train for the capital city, Colombo, where he was to do some banking and return in time to purchase the vehicle and celebrate with his family. But it was there that things went horribly wrong.

Aiomi told me that she did not know exactly what Clement was doing at the bank. In their culture, that was a man's business and so she had no interest or need to know at the time. What she did know was that he was scheduled to arrive home in the early evening. The family arrived but he did not. They waited and waited and then came a knock at the door.

The police were there to break the bad news. They found Clement's body next to the railroad tracks that brought him from Colombo to their village. During their investigation to determine whose body it was, they searched his pockets. Along with his address they found a train ticket. It was that ticket that told the sad story.

In Clement's excitement to return home that evening he bought a ticket and boarded the express train rather than the local train that stops in their village. They surmise that he realized his mistake while the train clattered down the rickety tracks towards his village. He knew that if he passed by the village on the express train there was no way to get back to the village that evening. He knew that his extended family waited for him at home. He knew that if his mistake was discovered it would be an embarrassment, and in many Asian cultures saving face from embarrassment is a pursuit worth dying for. And apparently Clement did.

As the express train rolled through their village barely slowing to acknowledge its presence, Clement leapt from the train. Surely he meant to land softly and roll to safety. Neither happened. He died in that fall.

The news brought by the police struck Aiomi and she saw her world implode around her. Through the grief of dealing with the loss she still had to deal with caring for her children. She got a job teaching children. She was good at her job but bad at recovery.

Over the months that followed Clement's death Aiomi sank deeper and deeper into a spiritual and emotional black hole. She related to me that she felt that an impenetrable wall had been erected between her and God. Her grief was hers alone and she could not even speak to God, never mind hear from him.

Day after hard-working day and night after struggling night she plodded forward with questions that monopolized her thoughts. "God, where are you?" "God, why would you let this happen?" "God, how can I care for my children?" "God, will I ever be married again in this culture where there are almost no Christians and no one willing to marry a widow with three children?" "God, why me?" "God, what now?"

Over time, the questions about God's dealings were replaced with answers about God's person. Yes, God was good. Yes, God did still love her with an everlasting love. Yes, God's promises to care for her and her children were as true as when Clement lived.

Brick by brick, the wall she felt separating herself from God came down and the warmth of his love and healing enveloped her, replacing the ice of her frozen faith. The magnitude of God's care for her expressed in the Scriptures, in her Christian friends, and in her spirit led to a healing of her soul that she could not have imagined when the police knocked on the door.

But, that last question still remained: "God, what now?"

It was with that question ringing in her heart that Aiomi returned to church for the first time in nearly a year, on Christmas Day of 2004. The specific question that she was asking was this, "Lord, you came to earth and suffered for me. You have allowed me to suffer and have brought your love and healing to my heart. You have allowed me to be a widow with children. Now, how are you going to use me as a widow for your glory?"

The answer came swiftly—as swiftly as the tsunami waves that reached her island just before 8 o'clock the next morning. An earthquake deep in the ocean floor near the Indonesian Island of Sumatra had created such turmoil in the Indian Ocean that tsunami waves raced nearly 1,000 miles in two hours and washed up onto the Sri Lankan shore just as thousands of men prepared for their fishing workday.

Over 30,000 people were killed and another 20,000 were injured on Sri Lanka alone. Immediately, Aiomi was face-to-face with thousands of women who were suddenly widows with small children and did not know how they could survive. Their worlds were shattered and they did not know where they could turn.

But Aiomi did.

And so she began serving those women and children who found that their homes and lives were seemingly destroyed.

And that brought us to the refugee camp where I sat on the hard bench and listened to Aiomi share her story and Jesus' story with the women.

And it was there that I needed that kick in the pants.

As I sat and listened to Aiomi's simple words, I thought to myself, "I am theologically trained. I have a great message on suffering—why God allows it and some of the benefits that could happen as a result. It has well-articulated points and Scripture verses and illustrative stories."

And then it hit me like a tsunami. From whom are these women more likely to receive a message on God's care for the suffering—from me or from Aiomi? If I were to share my self-evaluated brilliant message on suffering, these women wouldn't be receptive to me. I don't know suffering. We all knew that. A short time after that meeting in the camp I was going to hop on a plane and fly my way back to the richest and freest country in the world. To paraphrase the Scriptures, my light and momentary afflictions are not worth comparing with what they have gone through.

40

But, when Aiomi spoke, the women sat with hearts captured by her transparency and riveted to the truth that she shared. When Aiomi said, "I have suffered and I have found God's love conquers all of my pain and hurt. And let me tell you how you can experience his love...," they knew that she knew what they were feeling and offered the hope they were craving.

And once again I learned what I already knew: that indigenous, national Christians can reach their own country with the love of God and the Good News of Jesus Christ far better than I can.

For pictures of Aiomi and more information about Worldlink, please go to www.worldlinkonline.org.

Martyred on a Mission:
Vijay's Story

On June 13, 2016, Vijay died his second death.

In the darkness of a moonlit, mountainous dirt road in Central India, Vijay was ambushed and macheted to death, and his body was thrown over a cliff and into a rocky ravine.

This eruption of intense hatred came as Vijay was returning alone from a time of sharing the intense love of Christ with remote villagers. He, his wife, Vijaya, and a few Christians had traveled miles to visit the village on market day. They knew that this was a strategic time when the crowds from the region's smaller huts and hamlets would swell the center of the largest area village. Almost everyone from miles around would be there in the market that day. As the apostle Paul had often done in first-century Asia and Europe (see Acts 17:17), the small mission team shared the Good News of Jesus with the crowds in the marketplace. The motivation was the same as Paul's, too: "He was greatly distressed to see that the city was full of idols" (Acts 17:16).

Indeed, that town and the surrounding Koya tribal area was also filled with idols. As the Joshua Project notes:

The Koya practice their own ethnic religion, but also worship a number of Hindu gods and goddesses. Many Koya deities are female, the most important being the "mother earth."

Sacrifices are carried out by the village priests. The Koya do not believe in heaven, hell, or reincarnation. When a person dies, his body is carried on a cot which is covered with grain, liquor, new clothes, money, and a cow's tail. At the appropriate place, the cot is faced towards the West, and the body is burned. The ashes are placed in a clay pot. The Koya believe that their spirits either linger about the clay ancestor pot, patrol the sky over the village, or wander about the village disturbing daily life.

Vijay and Vijaya had moved with their two young daughters (ages 7 and 9) to that remote region two years earlier because they knew that the Koya tribe was virtually unreached with the Gospel. Almost 1,000,000 Koya tribal people live in villages straddling the Godavari river. And, though the river offers water, they had no way of knowing about the living water that Jesus offered.

As he walked the earth, Jesus, knowing that there were many people in Samaria who needed living water, made a radical choice recorded in John 4. In verse 4 it says, "he had to go through Samaria." While physically he could have avoided Samaria, while culturally he should have avoided Samaria, while emotionally it would have been easier to avoid Samaria, Jesus "had to go" through that area. He knew that unreached people awaited and his heart compelled him to be with them.

Vijay and Vijaya had to go to the tribal area because the unreached Koya people awaited and their hearts compelled them.

For two years they lived in a bamboo hut on rented land and toiled to serve the Koya people they loved with the love of the

Lord. They brought electricity to the village… along with the power of the Holy Spirit. They brought pumped water to the village… along with the water of life. They loved and served the people even while a radical group in the area opposed them. They gave their lives to the Koya as they had previously given their lives to Jesus.

That is why I said that Vijay died his second death. He had died, in Christ, years before. He had abandoned his life to live for Christ. He was in the village as a dead man preaching. He knew the truth of Paul's statement: "For Christ's love compels us, because we are convinced that one died for all, and therefore all died. And he died for all, that those who live should no longer live for themselves but for him who died for them and was raised again" (2 Corinthians 5:14-15). In fact, Vijaya commented about her husband at his memorial service that, "My husband's desire was to be a martyr and he was influenced by the ministry and life of brother Graham Staines and family. God fulfilled his desire."

Suku, the leader of Worldlink's partners in that area, wrote to me after the memorial service. He said:

Dear Brother,

Thank you for your prayers. We have no words to say how God had taken us through a deep forest to meet our dear sister Vijaya, her girls, and the church. It was a long 6-hour journey to the village nearing the border of the states Chatisgarh and Orissa.

There were above 500 people gathered for giving thanks to God for Mr. Vijay's life and ministry. The program was coordinated by the local Brethren Assembly as Vijay's elder brother is also a Missionary in the nearby area for the past 20 years.

He not only preached Gospel to the unreached but also brought electricity and a water pump to the village. The whole village was moved and the village head (animist—he never believed Gospel) gave open testimony about Vijay's love for the people through social development and lifestyle as a good human being and also he added that, "this person (Vijay) could do it because he was a Christian." Thank God.

We spend time with Mrs. Vijaya, her daughters and family members. They are broken beyond our words.

According to them...

Mr. Vijay and family along with a few believers went to hold a Gospel meeting. They distributed tracts and held open air meetings... He went by motor bike and sent back his family and believers by bus. He bought rice and mats for the church and was returning through the usual mountain pass road to reach his village. He had to drive around 145 kms and crossed 75 kms and left 70 to reach home. There it happened that jungle robbers attacked him suspecting he was a merchant returning after selling his products in the nearby market.

Nobody had seen what had happened. So we can't say anything about the incident how and why. Police were informed by someone on the next day. They had conducted postmortem and clearly stated it is a murder. The investigation is going on. No clues until now...

I think most of your questions are answered. I know there is no clarity about why they killed him. We can only suspect as there are no witness. Few people also suspect anti-Christian forces because his Bible was crumbled. We don't know but God delighted *in his short life and Vijay is with him. His story is a challenge to the rest of the Christian world. We expect great breakthrough in and around these villages through his death.*

With mixed emotion of deep grief and joy of his life in Christ,

Suku & Jessy

There are only a few who know the exact reason why Vijay was targeted. God knows, but he has not chosen to tell us. The murderers know, but they are not confessing.

Whether Vijay was targeted because of his faith and service, or was just in the dangerous area because of his faith and service makes little difference. Vijay would not have been murdered if he were not a Christian on a mission.

Vijay's mission is the same one that belongs to each of us who are Christians: to share God's love and Good News with those who have never heard.

I last saw Vijay and Vijaya just seven months earlier at a conference held to encourage our indigenous missionary partners in Andhra Pradesh. On the last day of the conference the local church had arranged a baptism. Vijaya was on the steps of the pool helping the newly believing women with wraps as they came out of the water. Vijay was nearby with the men. They were serving again, giving themselves again. Now, a few months later, Vijay is resting.

We Rest on Thee

In 1895, two years before her death at 25 years old, Edith Cherry wrote a poem called "We Rest on Thee." It was published in a collection of her poems that were later assembled by Edith's mother, and subsequently it was put to music and became a beloved hymn sung by millions of Christians. The fame of the poem's simple words of devotion and commitment to serving Christ exploded when it was revealed that it was the last song sung by five men in 1956 before they entered the Ecuadorian jungle to bring the Gospel to another unreached tribe, the Acua. Having put themselves in harm's way but in God's hands, these five men were murdered on the banks of the Curaray River and their bodies discovered days later.

The martyrdom of these five men crushed families and coworkers and shocked many who never knew them. Inspired by their sacrifice, a new army of Christians rose up to follow their footsteps with a new passion to bring the Good News of Jesus Christ to those who had never heard of him.

In a similar way, it is my fervent prayer that the Lord will use the horrible yet beautiful, cowardly yet brave, evil yet good, crushing yet inspiring death of Vijay to ignite in the hearts of all who hear of him a flame of passion to reach the unreached Koya along with the over 2,000 unreached tribes in India and many thousands more around the world. That some would pick up the fallen baton of a fallen brother and continue to run the race set before them in front-line indigenous missionary service to unreached people. That some, knowing that their part is not to live in a hut and reach villagers but to provide resources for those who can, might so rearrange their priorities as to free up much more of God's money to do God's mission in reaching the unreached. That some, knowing that their only resource is in their heart and voice, might storm the throne of heaven in agonizing and tearful pleading for God's current and future missionaries who will be the conduit of living water to the spiritually parched.

As I write, my heart is hurting. Hurting for the loss of a partner in ministry. Hurting for his family in confusion and need. Hurting for the team who will continue without him. Hurting for the sin-blinded men who snatched his life. Hurting for the people in darkness who need a new missionary like Vijay to bring light.

But, stronger than that hurt is a clear resolve. Vijay's life was an example and his death was an alarm. I don't know how long the Lord will allow me to continue this mission, but as long as he gives me another moment, I pray for the strength to live like Vijay and the grace to die like Vijay in the service of the One and Only Savior and for the sake of those who have not heard.

We must, inspired by Vijay's life and death, double or triple our efforts to add more and more indigenous missionaries to more and more countries to reach more and more unreached. When God raises up a person to go back to the Koya in Vijay's place, Worldlink must be there. When God calls new indigenous men and women to be missionaries to reach out to their own people, Worldlink must be there. When the next wave of hundreds of indigenous missionaries step out to put their lives on the line for the Lord and his ministry, Worldlink must be there.

Vijay's legacy deserves no less.

I have asked myself often, "Is it more difficult to give your life in a singular act of heroic self-sacrifice for others, or to give your life in a continual, moment by moment, day by day, year after year lifestyle of self-sacrificial love for the good of others?"

While I was musing on those things, Vijay was living them. God give me the strength to do the same.

How can we who remain do any less?

I leave you with the words of Edith Cherry's poem-turned hymn. Vijay rested his life on his Shield and Defender. He went with Christ into the battle against the foe. On June 13, Vijay did not return home from the battle. Instead, still resting on Christ, he passed through the gates of pearly splendor and rests with his Jesus through endless days.

Rest well, my friend, rest well!

We Rest on Thee

We rest on Thee, our Shield and our Defender!
We go not forth alone against the foe;
Strong in Thy strength, safe in Thy keeping tender,
We rest on Thee, and in Thy Name we go.
Strong in Thy strength, safe in Thy keeping tender,
We rest on Thee, and in Thy Name we go.

Yes, in Thy Name, O Captain of salvation!
In Thy dear Name, all other names above;
Jesus our Righteousness, our sure Foundation,
Our Prince of glory and our King of love.
Jesus our Righteousness, our sure Foundation,
Our Prince of glory and our King of love.

We go in faith, our own great weakness feeling,
And needing more each day Thy grace to know:
Yet from our hearts a song of triumph pealing,

"We rest on Thee, and in Thy Name we go."
Yet from our hearts a song of triumph pealing,
"We rest on Thee, and in Thy Name we go."

We rest on Thee, our Shield and our Defender!
Thine is the battle, Thine shall be the praise;
When passing through the gates of pearly splendor,
Victors, we rest with Thee, through endless days.
When passing through the gates of pearly splendor,
Victors, we rest with Thee, through endless days.

For pictures of Vijay and more information about Worldlink,
please go to www.worldlinkonline.org.

Innovation:
A Personal Shopper's Story

I sat with a group of young men who would soon thereafter become Worldlink partners in an Islamic country that I will not name. As I often do, I had the privilege of listening to the story of their lives, their calling into ministry, and their unique strategies to reach their countrymen for Christ.

I had just traveled around their country and saw firsthand the difficulty that they would face as they attempted to strike spiritual conversations with people in the surrounding villages. The villagers were staunchly religious, very isolated, and notoriously suspicious of outsiders. They were standoffish toward people from other villages and hostile toward those from other countries. One young man had developed a strategy that at first confused me, then amused me, and lastly astonished me. He said that he was a "Personal Shopper."

I knew that there were no department stores within 100 miles, so I assumed he meant something different than what I was thinking. He did.

He explained. He had a motorbike and so he rode up into the hills to the remote villages. He would ask people what they needed from the larger towns. One might need a box of nails. Another might need a shirt. Another might need some medicine.

Having taken the orders, he would ride his motorcycle many kilometers to the nearest bigger town with a market. He would purchase the items requested and bring them back to the village. Then the unique strategy really started.

Instead of requiring the man to pay two dollars for the box of nails, our young missionary friend would ask him to pay 20 cents a week for the next 10 weeks. This would give him 10 opportunities to begin a friendship, develop a relationship, and ultimately steer a conversation to the Good News of Jesus Christ.

Those 10 conversations gave our friend the chance to eliminate the notorious suspicion of outsiders that characterize those tribes. After several months, he was no longer an outsider. He was a friend and someone respected because he did business and served his customers well. He honored his commitments, and that spoke volumes.

The results? Many people heard about Jesus. Some people rejected the young man and his message. Some were curious and wanted to talk more even after full payment was made. Some opened their hearts to the young man who brought the nails and to the man who was nailed to the cross for them.

For pictures of indigenous missionaries and more information about Worldlink, please go to www.worldlinkonline.org.

Living Water:
Shankar's Story

God is amazing and his amazing power is changing lives around the world!

Shankar's story is one example of God's power. I met Shankar three years ago in a village in India, and I saw him there again last month. The change in his life brought tears to my eyes.

Three years ago, God provided the $3,000 that was required to purchase a piece of property in central India. This property was to be the site of a Children's Home that would bring life to a group of orphaned, abandoned, and abused children. I had seen the property before because it is adjacent to a church that is led by Suku and Jessy, Worldlink partners and area leaders.

The church, as well as Suku and Jessy's home, did not have running water, which would be critical to a children's home for obvious reasons. So God provided the funds to dig a borehole well on the new property.

That's where Phase I of God's amazing work in Shankar's life began.

I arrived in their village the day after the well was dug, and we saw clean, fresh, life-giving water flowing out.

As I sat in Suku and Jessy's small house with open doors and windows, Shankar, their neighbor, approached. He wore a Dhoti, a traditional cotton wrapped skirt, with a dirty shirt and bare feet.

He was a Hindu and worshipped the images that he kept in his small home. Shankar asked if he could tell me something. Of course he could!

Shankar said, "I have lived in this village, next to this property all of my life. Many people have tried to dig wells here. They prayed and sacrificed to their many gods and dug time after time but they never got the water. But I watched as you all came and prayed to your God and dedicated the land to him and when you dug you got water. I think that is a miracle!"

I told him, "I think you're right!"

Shankar continued, "I think your God is very strong!"

I echoed again, "I think you're right!" And then I added, "Keep watching this property, because you are going to see bigger miracles than water that gives physical life. You'll see a home rise up that gives love and life to many children."

I was so excited that Shankar was beginning to see God's power, love, and grace. And I prayed that the Lord would continue to open his eyes.

Over the next three years, God did just that. I was there again two years ago as the Children's Home was dedicated and the kids arrived. I didn't note it then, but Shankar watched from the front of his nearby hut. And he continued to watch.

Unseen by me, as my attention went to the ministry of Worldlink's other indigenous missionary partners, Suku and Jessy kept showing Shankar the true God's love and power and grace.

They spoke of the God whose love was shown when he sent a Savior to die for Shankar's sin. The God whose power was proven when he raised Christ from the dead. The God whose grace offers Shankar "living water" which will satisfy the deep longing of his soul and never leave him spiritually thirsty again.

Last month, I returned to visit with Suku and Jessy and to meet with about 50 of Worldlink's indigenous missionary partners in India and nearby countries. With joyous celebration the growing church on the property was having a baptism whereby recent converts could publicly proclaim that they had turned from all of the things that they previously worshipped, to trust in Jesus Christ alone as the forgiver of their sins and the leader of their lives.

As I and a crowd of others (including the rescued children from the children's home) watched, person after person climbed into the small baptismal pool filled with water from the well.

My heart swelled. My mind raced. My eyes moistened as Shankar mounted the small concrete steps and gave witness to his new faith in Jesus by receiving baptism.

I looked over at Jessy and she hid her face and quietly wept for the joy of seeing Shankar take this huge step.

"Lord," I thought, "why do you allow me to see such amazing work that you're doing around the world though our partners?" I think he allows me to see the stories so that I can tell the stories. Stories that demonstrate that people are reachable.

For pictures of Shankar and more information about Worldlink, please go to www.worldlinkonline.org.

How Can I Leave Them?: Kiran's Story

"How can I leave them there, when Jesus did not leave me there?" It was a simple question but the story behind it makes it profound.

I studied his face intently as Kiran asked the question. His brow showed the face of a man who felt that the answer was self-evident. Yet even asking the question and contemplating its assumed answer left Kiran's eyes moist and his lip quivering. To understand why you must understand Kiran.

Kiran is one of Worldlink's indigenous missionary partners and an area leader. He is highly educated with Bachelor of Arts and Bachelor of Theology degrees, Master of Divinity and Master of Theology degrees, and is studying for his PhD in Philosophy and World Religions.

Kiran knows several languages, and his quick mind and obvious passion make him one of my all-time favorite translators as he accompanies me on most of my trips in central India.

Kiran and his wife, Beulah, both have a heart for God, a heart for those unreached with the news of Jesus, and a heart for orphaned, abused, and abandoned children. They have taken eight children off the streets and into their home.

If you think that his life now is the natural result of his upbringing, you would be wrong.

Kiran was born and raised in an Orthodox Hindu family. But not just any common family—his was a Brahmin family. His was the upper caste of Indian society —the priestly caste. And instilled in him and his sister from an early age was a hunger for seeking to please the gods.

His mother was very devoted to following all of the proper Hindu customs and rituals. Because of her pious nature she rose to serve as a priestess in a Hindu temple and Kiran served as the assistant priest. As such, he was compelled to assist in the daily rituals and to learn the Hindu scriptures. So serious was his mother that if Kiran did not perform his duties and memorize his passages each morning he was not given food.

Hunger can be a tremendous motivator. Kiran rose early each morning. By 4:30 a.m. he awoke and began to wash the idols to make them ready for the day's sacrifices. His passionate devotion to his religion was accompanied by an equally passionate disgust toward Christ and Christians.

Kiran's mother and he mocked Christians who mostly were from the lower caste of Indian society. He took whatever opportunity he could to ridicule Jesus, even though he knew very little about him. His persecution of Christians was a combination of historical ignorance, religious fear, and social snobbery. Fueled by these sources and encouraged by those around him, he nurtured a deep hatred for Christianity.

About the time that Kiran was 10 years old some major changes began to happen in his extended family. Kiran's grandmother, who was an upper caste landowner in their home village, became the target of people who wished to take her land. One by one his aunts and uncles and family members were killed.

His mother was the only remaining heir. Ultimately, although his mother was not killed, the family lost the ancestral property.

This caused them to multiply their efforts to appease their gods and seek the restoration of the property and retribution on those who took it. They visited several Hindu holy sites and offered sacrifices to satisfy the wrath of the gods and goddesses that they felt allowed this injustice. But there was no relief. They consulted sorcerers and witch doctors to access spiritual powers. But there was no relief. They took pilgrimages to faraway temples. But there was no relief. They prayed for the help of gods or demons to inflict the others, but Kiran found that he was the one becoming afflicted.

Kiran explained that every new moon day he would "shout and cry loudly and run away from home and used to walk the roads like a mad fellow." His parents and the police sought him regularly and found him lying beside roadways incoherent. Let me allow him to share in his own words (remember, English is not his first or second language) what happened next:

> I was only 12 years old. My parents took me to different witch doctors in order to make me get rid of those demonic powers. But those witch doctors also could not help me. They did lot of sacrifices for me; they used to cut hen and goat and used to pour that blood in order to satisfy the demons. They used to tie different threads by telling that demon will not come back. But nothing happened. As a result I became worse. My father used to carry me on his shoulder and used to beg all the priests and witch doctors to cure me from evil spirits. But there was none to help me.

It was 1999 September 17. I don't know what was happening and I completely lost my control. I tear my school dress and threw my shoes one side and threw my bicycle somewhere and started walking on the roads. I began to sleep beside roads, railway stations, bus stations and eat from garbage cans and trash boxes.Witchcraft powers and evil spirits always used to motivate me to end my life by jumping from advertisement boards and used to harm my body by cutting myself. I used to sleep beside dustbins nearby railway station in order to get some food.

Like that I suffered 3 years not remembering my parents or anyone. I was completely out of my mind not knowing where I am going, what I was doing. As it happened one day during Child Labour Survey, an orphan home nearby railway station, began to search for orphan children and found me lying beside the road. My both hands were almost eaten by scabies and about to die. I was on my death bed. I was unable to walk and speak any word. But they took me to their orphan home and took care of me. By seeing my situation they felt pity and used to give bath to me and used to feed food to me because I was completely out of my mind. Since I forgot everything, that Christian orphan home father gave my name as Kiran Kumar. He used to daily pray for me.

Simultaneously, and unknown to each other, while Kiran's life began the slow assent from the pits, his mother's life took a radical turn.

After 23 years of following and serving the idols, and three intense years of praying for her lost son, Kiran's mother was confronted with the claims and the person of Jesus Christ. She responded in faith to his love and became a Christian.

Her conversion was immediately greeted by her family with the same hatred that she had spewed on Christians in the past. She was scolded, beaten, and ostracized by the society. Her family was banished from the Hindu temple and from the village community. Neighbors began to taunt her saying that her departure from the idols meant that her son was dead and would never come home again. Kiran's mother stood steadfast during these trials and eventually her faith and witness led her husband and daughter to put their faith in Jesus.

Kiran's mother asked the few local Christians to pray for Kiran's deliverance and return. They prayed and fasted and cried out to God. And God answered in a very special way.

Over the months, as the three people who loved him and many more who had never met him prayed for Kiran, he experienced the deliverance and return to health for which they asked. But being reunited to his family was another miracle.

After the December 2004 Tsunami in the Indian Ocean, the children of the Children's Home where Kiran was living were sent to the streets to request contributions that were to be used to provide relief for the suffering Indians on the coast. "Coincidentally," Kiran's mom and sister had gone to this different city to do some shopping.

There, on the street, they were approached by a clean-cut, well-behaved, articulate young man asking for contributions. They instantly recognized each other and the prayed-for reunion was complete. After thanking those who had cared for him, Kiran left the Children's Home and returned to his family home.

It was there that the explanations of what the true God had done to deliver and restore him physically and emotionally and the explanation of what Jesus had done on the cross to deliver and restore him spiritually finally made sense. Kiran placed his faith in Christ, and joy overwhelmed him as he realized that the closeness with God that he had wanted to find and worked to find all his life was now offered to him simply by faith.

It was the realization that Jesus had not left him on the streets abandoned and alone, and that Jesus had not left him in his sin lost and alone, that led Kiran to commit his life to rescuing those who currently are lost or left as he was.

Whether it is an orphaned, abused, or abandoned child on the street or a person struggling to find forgiveness, Kiran can't help but serve them. If you ask him why, he will give you the same answer he gave me: "How can I leave them there, when Jesus did not leave me there?"

For pictures of Kiran and more information about Worldlink, please go to www.worldlinkonline.org.

All of Them:
Suman's Story

He looks more like an accountant than a hero. Wait—now that I think of it, I know several CPAs who are pretty heroic, so let me rephrase that first sentence.

He looks more like the comical characterization of an accountant than a hero. Suman wears a slightly baggie and threadbare short-sleeve dress shirt with one too many pens in the drooping pocket. His polyester dress pants are hiked a bit higher than seems comfortable. But, when nobody is looking, I imagine that his shirt comes off revealing a giant "S" for Superman on his chest and a flowing red cape is revealed.

He lives in a South Asian country in which less than one-half of 1% of the population is Christians. He was born, raised, and grew up into his late teens in a tribe that lived in a rural, hilly, forested area several hours from any city. Everyone in his village and in the surrounding villages of his tribe was loosely related to each other from generations back. If you were in the little school, you were with people you knew and were related to. When you needed a job, it was likely provided by some near or distant relation. When your parents thought it was time for you to marry, they chose your mate from the pool of candidates whom they knew well because they were from the same tribe. Everyone Suman knew was in the same tribe and everyone he knew was, at least nominally, in the same religion, because everyone in his tribe was assumed to be in their tribal faith. He did not feel forced. Nobody needed to force anyone to choose because there was only one choice.

Suman's tribe had zero Christians and so Suman knew zero Christians and so Suman had zero knowledge of Christ's message. When he was 16, he first heard the name Jesus, but he knew nothing about him.

Showing great intellectual promise, Suman left his tribe for a larger city to get his education. There he was confronted with many new experiences: new options in living conditions; new transportation options; new food options; new thought options.

It was there at college that he heard, for the second time, the name Jesus. He met a local Christian pastor and they began to talk. Over a short time, he learned more. He saw the contrast between the daily rituals and meditations that he had done for his whole life that left him still acutely aware of his sin and Jesus' once-for-all-time sacrifice for sin and offer of full and forever forgiveness. He saw the contrast between the powerlessness that he felt in his life that left him unable to live as his religion told him he should and the power that his new Christian friend experienced in his life. Suman poured over the Bible and God's Spirit made it come alive to him. Ultimately, he accepted Jesus as his Savior at age 20.

Suman's heart broke because he knew that nobody in his tribe in the forested villages had ever heard of Christ or ever experienced this life he was now enjoying. But when he went back to share with them, they violently opposed him and his Savior. Now his heart was doubly broken.

Suman could not answer the questions posed by his friends and relatives. He felt the need for some further education and just wanted to follow and serve Jesus. He joined a local team of Christians and was trained. He then served in children's ministry for several years in a distant city. He began planting churches and serving as a pastor. But his heart was still burdened for his family and tribe.

Through the generosity of a man from a neighboring country, Suman was able to attend a Bible college in that country. He studied hard and received his Master of Divinity degree at the age of 31. By then, the call to return to his tribe full-time was stronger than ever.

Suman returned to share God's love and the Good News with his tribe. It has not been all smooth sailing. The Bible quite clearly promises that "Everyone who wants to live a godly life in Christ Jesus will be persecuted" (2 Timothy 3:12). Jesus warned his followers to, "Remember what I told you: 'A servant is not greater than his master.' If they persecuted me, they will persecute you also. If they obeyed my teaching, they will obey yours also" (John 15:20).

In his Olivet Discourse, Jesus told his disciples that before the prophesied events at the end of the age come, "They will seize you and persecute you. They will hand you over to synagogues and put you in prison, and you will be brought before kings and governors, and all on account of my name" (Luke 21:12). Suman knew of these promises in his head and he had experienced their reality.

Because of his faith in Jesus, Suman was rejected by his family and tribe. He had been offered no job. His parents would not arrange a marriage. He could not live at home. Because of the beatings he endured, he was forced to move to a city several hours from his village. But, because of his love for his people, he continued to visit the villages.

His strategy was to talk to the young people whom he knew were struggling like he was at their age and asking the same questions he was at their age.

The fruit of his ministry over the past few years includes over 30 young men between 14 and 25 years old who have come to understand who Jesus is, what he did, and what he offers them and have accepted Jesus as their savior. I met these young men in a town where they live about a two-hour drive from their villages.

Why do they live away from their families? Because they, too, have been rejected by their families and community. They are experiencing what Suman did earlier. But, I must tell you, I cannot remember seeing a group of more joyous Christians anywhere in the 50-plus countries I have visited. They have lost much, but they have gained much more.

They have formed a small "Bible Institute." They live and study there and most are studying their academic subjects too. The Bible Institute consists of two small 10x14-foot rooms off a dark, narrow alley in the town. In one room are plastic stacking chairs where they study the Bible and learn to know Jesus and make him known. That room also serves as the dormitory. In the evening, the boys stack the chairs, grab a blanket from a pile, wrap up, and sleep on the cold, hard concrete floor.

In the other room is the small two-burner propane stove on which they cook their daily meal of rice and a few vegetables (and only occasionally meat). It also contains the one bookshelf that is the Bible Institute's library, and the four-foot rod that serves as the "closet" for all of the clothes that they are not wearing.

They may have lost the comforts of home, but in their new home they are experiencing the joy of seeing God's provision of what they say they really need to live.

They may have lost (they pray that it is temporary) the family and community of their upbringing, but the Christian brotherhood of their new community is providing a family that they say is closer than any they have ever experienced before.

They may currently have no father or relatives who will offer them work when they finish school, but they do not worry about tomorrow because their Heavenly Father has given them confidence in his ability to provide.

There is one area, though, that these young men discussed with me in tones that evidence an understandable unease. That is their future marriage prospects. Because of their faith, their parents will not pursue a wife for them from their tribe. For the same reason, no parent would give their daughter in marriage to these young men. Further, they will only marry believers in Jesus, and that narrows the options to almost none.

But God has been doing a quiet work lately. Over the past couple of years, as these 30 young men have gone back covertly into their home villages and shared the Good News of Jesus with their friends, an equal number of young women have come to the faith. But they must remain "secret believers" because of the persecution. If the girls' parents discovered that they had come to faith in Jesus they would quickly marry them off to men in the village.

We spent a good amount of time talking about this situation. The young men have laid this matter at the feet of their Heavenly Father and are trusting him for their future mates as they have for everything else in their futures. They are concentrating now on knowing Jesus and making him known.

Of Suman's first disciples, six of these young people have become the next generation of indigenous missionaries reaching their tribal villages. They are passionately in love with and committed to Jesus. They want others to be the same. I am humbled to be their friend and partner.

The experience of these frontline first-generation Christians parallels the experience of the early New Testament church as they brought the Good News to people who had never been heard.

Remember Jesus had said that, "They will seize you and persecute you. They will hand you over to synagogues and put you in prison, and you will be brought before kings and governors, and all on account of my name." That very thing happened to Jesus' early followers.

In Acts 4, Peter and John were seized by the religious/cultural officials because they were teaching people about Jesus. Peter and John were put in prison and, the next day, were given a chance to explain their teaching. Filled with the Holy Spirit, they gave clear defense of their faith in Christ.

It was at that point that we read: "When they saw the courage of Peter and John and realized that they were unschooled, ordinary men, they were astonished and they took note that these men had been with Jesus" (Acts 4:13). The simple and courageous faith of uneducated and ordinary people so confounded the learned leaders that it gave clear evidence that they had been with Jesus.

That same thing is happening today. On May 26, 2016, five of the remarkable young Christian men whom I had met were hauled before their village leaders, with many people watching, to give a defense of their new Christian faith that they were sharing in the villages. It could have gone horribly wrong and led to great persecution.

I received an urgent prayer request from Suman when he heard that the boys were summoned. He wrote (I will share his exact words although English is not his native language): "We are all praying for these five that they may able to stand with the power of the Holy Spirit to their village people and praying for God's glory to reveal among that village people."

We all prayed and God answered.

After the meeting, Suman wrote to me:

The meeting was good. Their discussion was also good, though the villages people don't want to adopt Christianity right now, still some people was positive in Christianity and as well our five Christian brother has spoked by humility with them... I believe that God is working and helping us. These are happening because of your kindness prayer. Thank you so much for your loving kindness prayer.

Again, in our age, the simple and courageous faith of ordinary people so confounded the leaders that it gave clear evidence that they had been with Jesus. Simple Christians living with Jesus and serving him is what Worldlink is all about.

Did you notice what Suman said about the villagers? They "don't want to adopt Christianity *right now*." That is a hope-filled and faith-filled statement echoed by so many of our frontline missionaries. They believe that the day will come when their tribe will not only hear the Good News and not only realize that others have been with Jesus, but they will know and experience the truth of what Peter shared at his hearing in Acts 4:12: "Salvation is found in no one else, for there is no other name under heaven given to men by which we must be saved."

In fact, one of the young missionaries in Suman's group told me that his prayer is that his tribe would be 100% Christian. That is my prayer, too! That's what we are working toward together.

For pictures of Suman and more information about Worldlink, please go to www.worldlinkonline.org.

Where You Cannot Go, I Will Go for You: Dickens's Story

Dickens and I sat in a sweltering room in Kampala, Uganda, talking about his life, his ministry, and his upcoming marriage. Around us sat half a dozen teenage young men whom Dickens was training to be ministers.

In their culture, Dickens explained, he, as the prospective groom, was expected to bring to his prospective in-laws a "brideprice." He showed me the list of items. It included, among many other things, clothing, bags, a farm animal, and a list of food that looked to me to be sufficient to feed a small village.

I knew that this would be very expensive. Dickens explained that he would enlist a group of respected friends (pastors, teachers, relatives, clan leaders...) to come with him in a procession from his village to his wife's home and each of these people would assure his wife's parents that Dickens was a respectable and honorable man worthy of caring for their daughter. Each of these friends will take part of the list to bring. When they arrive they would join his wife's family and village to celebrate the engagement with a giant meal with the food that they brought.

I joked that maybe I should attempt to instill this practice in our culture, seeing that I have two daughters.

A short time later, we all piled into the back of a truck to drive to a school where Dickens and his team would present a Christian outreach program. As we bounced along the dirt roads, one of the teens innocently asked me about my daughters' ages. His colleagues set upon him like a pack of laughing lions sensing a vulnerable target. "You could never afford the bride price for Uncle Jack's daughters! He wouldn't want a goat; he would want a Land Rover!" From there, their estimated bride price only grew and the curious young man was repeatedly reminded, with increasingly louder laughter, that he was trying to play out of his league. By the time they ended, I think they had raised the price to include several palaces and an airliner!

Good-natured kidding and laughter seemed to transcend our different cultures (although the Land Rover didn't seem like such a bad idea). Another thing that transcended our cultures was the saving message of Jesus Christ that I saw Dickens and his young team present that day in the school we visited.

They did what I could not do. They brought the unchanging message of God's love in a language I did not speak and into a culture I did not understand. And the eternal results were far better than any material prize!

Since that day, I have watched Dickens grow in his family life and his ministry life. He has a beautiful family and a beautiful ministry. Dickens leads a team of Ugandan young people, both staff and volunteers, who are seeing thousands of Ugandans hear and respond to the same simple message of Jesus that they shared in that school years ago.

I treasure Dickens's partnership with Worldlink, and so does he. This is how he phrases it in a video recorded to address Worldlink supporters:

I am grateful for your support. Thank you, Worldlink, and every one of you out there who keeps us in prayer, who keeps us moving with your money. That money does much. Where I cannot go your money has made me to go. And where you cannot go I will go for you when that money is there, when that prayer is there. Challenges might be there, but together we can make a difference for the Lord Jesus Christ.

Dickens's partnership is a treasure and yet not a totally unique treasure. We have hundreds of indigenous missionary partners like Dickens who can say to Christians in the West, "Where you cannot go, I will go for you."

I thank God for the prayer and support that makes it possible for indigenous missionaries to "go" and bring the love of God and Good News of Jesus to where you and I cannot go.

For pictures of Dickens and more information about Worldlink, please go to www.worldlinkonline.org.

The Light Shines Brightest: Sandra's Story

The joke is that Huehuetenango (pronounced way-way-tenango) is way, way up north in Guatemala. And it is more than a joke.

Every time that I have flown into Guatemala, after spending some time with partners in the area surrounding the capital, Guatemala City, a few partners and I make the six-hour ride up Central America Highway One (CA1) to "Huehue." There, I meet Sandra. She is a small woman with a big heart. It is unlikely that she comes close to 5 feet tall, which creates quite a sight next to my 6-foot-3-inch frame.

But what Sandra lacks in size, she more than makes up for in spirit. Sandra loves Jesus and loves children and works hard, so that her two loves blend together in beautiful harmony. She goes to local schools, parks, and churches and runs programs to introduce children to Jesus and to help them grow to know him better. She trains and supervises volunteers to multiply the ministry into as many corners of the region as she can. She is a tireless and fearless worker in an environment that would tire almost anyone and bring fear to the hearts of most people.

I always go to visit Sandra's ministry—except for once.

CA 1 is the main road that travels between Central America and the United States. Therefore, it is the central travel route for both drugs and humans to illegally enter the United States. Huchuetenango sits on the border between Guatemala and

Mexico. At the time of my planned visit, the team in Huehue communicated that it was unsafe for me to travel there. The drug cartels had begun a skirmish for control of the trade route. Many vehicles were being stopped and many people did not make it through. Both visitors and locals were disappearing.

So Sandra took a bus south and we met in Antigua. Antigua is a beautiful ancient city of remarkably well-preserved Baroque-style Spanish architecture. My original college major was architectural engineering, so I love seeing unique buildings around the world. Antigua was the former capital of the Kingdom of Guatemala and is now known for its tourism and Spanish-language immersion schools.

On a beautiful afternoon, Sandra and I sat in a park with a few partners and I asked her to share about her life and ministry since we had last met. I noticed that she looked tired, but I chalked it up to the long overnight bus ride. I soon found that it was much more than physical exhaustion.

Sandra relayed to me that her son had been shot to death just about a week earlier.

Her son had grown up with all the advantages of a loving home. But, as with too many who become teenagers in a rough, drug-riddled area, he had joined a gang. He left behind any pretense of following God and followed a group that led him in all the wrong directions. This broke his mother's heart, and the hearts of his physical father and his Heavenly Father.

None of them gave up on him. It was only a couple of years later, which seemed like an eternity, when her son showed up at home again. He was a broken young man whose heart had been brought to repentance and now wanted to reconcile with God and his parents.

Returning to his physical and spiritual roots was the easy part. His family and his Heavenly Father wanted him back with all their hearts. However, his gang did not want to let him go. They told him he must come back. No one leaves the gang. When that did not work, they promised him riches to return. When that did not work, they threatened to hurt him if he did not return. When that did not work, they promised to kill him if he did not return. He thought they were bluffing. They weren't.

On an unremarkable afternoon, Sandra's son stood on the street corner by their house speaking with his father. A motorcycle came down the road, just as hundreds do every hour. But this one stopped in the road a few feet from her son. In a spilt second, the man on the rear seat pulled out a gun and shot her son dead before the cycle roared off down the road.

Sandra's son died in the arms of his father that afternoon on the rough pavement of Huehuetenango. After he had breathed his last breath on earth he awoke in the arms of a different Father.

I cried with Sandra and prayed with Sandra. I imagined the horror for her family and the paralyzing effect this would have on her ministry.

It was horrible for the family, but what she said next shocked me. Contrary to my expectation, the ministry had been seeing more fruit than ever before.

Sandra told me how in the midst of the terrible times in their area, with the drug cartels battling and people being killed, and fear being felt on every street, the darkness of these circumstances was making the light of the Gospel shine even brighter.

She relayed to me that people were spiritually complacent when things were going well, but now that everything was falling apart around them in the midst of great uncertainty, they were now open to hear about a God who is certain.

Truly, it is in the midst of the darkest darkness that the Light shined the brightest.

Someone said, "It is better to light one candle than to curse the darkness." Sandra is lighting a bonfire.

For pictures of Sandra and more information about Worldlink, please go to www.worldlinkonline.org.

I want to be part of the team!

Because the unreached are REACHABLE, I want to help indigenous missionaries reach their countries for Christ. I understand that 100% of my sponsorship donation will go to my sponsored missionaries with nothing taken out for administrative expenses.

(Return this card or sponsor online at www.worldlinkonline.org)

[ ] Starting now, I will prayerfully sponsor:

_____ missionaries at $35 each month for a total of $ _____ /month

[ ] I already support a missionary and will prayerfully sponsor:

_____ additional missionaries at $35 each month for a total of $ _____ /month

[ ] I like someone from Worldlink to speak at my church/group

Please Print

Name _____

Address _____

City _____ State _____ Zip _____

Email _____

Phone _____

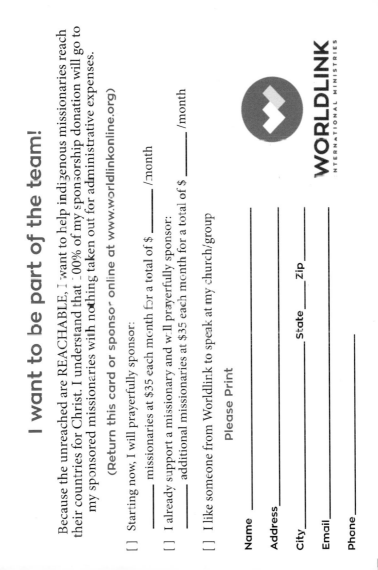

WORLDLINK
INTERNATIONAL MINISTRIES

Worldlink International Ministries
P.O. Box 80202, Valley Forge, PA 19484

Worldlink International Ministries
P.O. Box 80202
Valley Forge, PA 19484
USA

Place
Stamp
Here

Dedication:
Perpetua's Story

We arrived at Perpetua's home around mid-morning. The house was exceedingly modest by Western standards but quite nice by African standards. That means it had more than one room and was made out of block rather than bamboo or mud. For five days, I had been in the Democratic Republic of the Congo and I had seen no paved roads (except for the odd sight of a couple of hundred feet of pavement in front of a police station).

Perpetua's home was near the end of a dirt road, and as we bounced up the road I could hear the singing that was meant to greet us. The singing was by about 15 young girls who were victims of sexual violence and were being trained as seamstresses and who were offered healing and hope in Christ in Perpetua's house.

After greeting the girls and seeing the work that was going on, we hiked down the dirt road farther and into the fields where a new, larger brick building was under construction. This was to be the new home of the work of rescuing young girls and women. It sat on land donated by Perpetua and her husband. This land was from their ancestral inheritance, but having it for use in ministry was more important than having it for use by the family.

Such is the dedication I saw in Perpetua, and it was one of the reasons I was sure she would fit as a Worldlink partner. Since our partnership began, her ministry has grown and seen more fruit.

Recently I received Perpetua's quarterly report. In it, matter-of-factly, she lists her activities for the report period. As if it's nothing unusual, she relays that one of the things she is doing is: "Counseling traumatized widows and orphans (products of the massacre) and sharing the Gospel message with them."

Perhaps it is just normal service to her, but it is exceedingly unique and transforming to the women she is loving and serving in Christ's name. She tells one example of the results of her work when she says, "A traumatized woman had rejected the existence of God but she came to believe in Jesus Christ."

I remember thinking that Perpetua was aptly named as I watched her perpetual service.

For pictures of Perpetua and more information about
Worldlink, please go to www.worldlinkonline.org.

Part Two
We Are Worldlink

We Don't *Use* Nationals!

I stood there and listened as a familiar punch-in-the-gut tightness settled into my stomach. The words "We use nationals, too!" were so offensive to me, but I said nothing because I know that 30-second explanations usually arouse nothing but defensiveness.

The scene was one I know quite well. I have the privilege of preaching and teaching at churches, schools, and conferences quite often. I love teaching God's Word. I love informing people and inspiring them concerning what God is doing and could do through them to reach the unreached in our world. This was one of those occasions.

It was a "Missions Conference" with representatives of a dozen or more Western missionary agencies and individuals whom the host church had sent to far countries to do ministry. It was break time, and a group of us stood in the circle chatting. A couple from the church's congregation were engaging me in discussions of Worldlink's philosophy of ministry and our mission of bringing the love of God and the Good News of Jesus Christ to unreached people in partnership with indigenous missionaries. I had discussed the unique strategic advantages of partnering with national brothers and sisters in frontline evangelistic and church planting ministry. I was sharing some of the same types of remarkable stories of God's work that you read in this book.

And then it happened. One of the representatives of a traditional Western-sending mission agency jumped into the conversation and said, "We use nationals, too."

81

It was a punch to my gut!

What I wanted to shout was, "And THAT, my friend, is exactly the problem!"

At Worldlinik, we don't *use* nationals! We partner with indigenous, national, native Christians who want to be missionaries to their own people. We don't *use* them to do what *we* want them to do; we empower them to do what *they*, and we, believe *God* is calling them to do.

OK, you might think that the distinction is subtle. If so, try out this conversation. What if we were at a conference discussing outreach ministry to bring the Good News to people in the USA and the mission representative, talking about their organization's work in the inner-city, said, "We use black people, too!"

Subtle still?

Why We Support Indigenous Missionaries

My friend and colleague in ministry, Dr. CV John, and I both have our spiritual roots in a group of churches that tend to get great pleasure out of preaching outlines that are alliterated. So, unable to help ourselves, we came up with the following 10 reasons why we support the strategy of reaching the unreached through empowering partnerships with indigenous missionaries. Enjoy, all you alliteration lovers.

Indigenous missionaries are:

- **Sensitive Culturally**

  Indigenous missionaries understand the culture and the thinking of their own people and can apply the truth of God using (or avoiding) words, phrases, and illustrations that would be unknown to an outsider.

- **Superior Linguistically**

  While it would take two to five years for a foreigner to learn a new language and a lifetime to try to perfect it, indigenous missionaries can speak their local languages fluently and immediately.

- **Suited Educationally**

  Frontline outreach work in most of the world does not require the high educational standards of most Western missionary organizations. In fact, sometimes the simple truth of the Good News gets lost within educated speech and arguments. Simple local indigenous ministers are often ideally suited to serve simple local unreached people.

- **Stout Physically**

Local Christians are quite used to the difficult living and ministry conditions in which they serve because they grew up in those conditions.

- **Sympathetic Socially**

A local, indigenous missionary will live at the social/financial level of the people to whom they are bringing the Good News, creating a commonality and a resulting openness.

- **Secure Politically**

Indigenous missionaries will not be deported or denied entry because they are in their country of citizenship.

- **Simple Organizationally**

Organization of indigenous missionaries fits the simple cultural and relational norms of the local area without layers of complexity imposed from the outside.

- **Steadfast Passionately**

The local missionary has a passion to reach their own tribes and own country because they are his or her own "family."

- **Strong Spiritually**

Indigenous missionaries have some of the strongest faith in the world.

- **Sound Economically**

  Indigenous missionaries are remarkably cost-efficient because of their low salary needs, their ability to live in local-standard housing and eat local foods, their simple transportation needs while travelling on foot or by bike or public transport, and the lack of required international travel/insurance/visas or international education for their children.

Worldlink's Statement of Beliefs

We ask it all the time: "Why reinvent the wheel?" I try not to unless the wheel doesn't work.

When we started Worldlink, we needed a Statement of Beliefs that expressed our understanding of Scripture simply enough, yet completely enough, that everyone from the theologians on the board to the village church planters could understand and agree with. It was quite easy to find because I had been working for a decade with a ministry that had exactly that kind of statement.

So, with permission, we did not reinvent the Statement of Beliefs. We installed an identical one and started driving.

Worldlink International Ministries accepts and proclaims the historic truths of the Christian faith including the following:

God and the Human Race

We hold that the Lord our God is one: Father, Son, and Holy Spirit, and that he fulfils his sovereign purposes—in creation, revelation, redemption, judgment, and the coming of his kingdom—by the calling out from the world a people united to himself and to each other in love.

We acknowledge that though God made us in his own likeness and image, conferring on us dignity and worth and enabling us to respond to himself, we now are members of a fallen race; we have sinned and come short of his glory.

We believe that the Father has shown us his holy love in giving Jesus Christ, his only Son, for us, while through our sinfulness and guilt, we were subject to his wrath and condemnation; and has shown his grace by putting sinners right with himself when they place their trust in his Son.

We confess Jesus Christ as Lord and God; as truly human, born of the virgin Mary; as Servant, sinless, full of grace and truth; as only Mediator and Savior, dying on the cross in our place, representing us to God, redeeming us from the grip, guilt, and punishment of sin; as Victor over Satan and all his forces, rising from death with a glorious body, being taken up to be with his Father, one day returning personally in glory and judgment to establish his kingdom.

We believe in the Holy Spirit who convicts the world in regard to sin, righteousness, and judgment; who makes the death of Christ effective to sinners, declaring that they must now turn to Christ in repentance and directing their trust towards the Lord Jesus Christ; who through the new birth makes us partake in the life of the risen Christ, and who is present within all believers, illuminating their minds to grasp the truth of Scripture, producing in them his fruit, granting to them his gifts, and empowering them for service in the world.

The Scriptures

We believe that the Old and New Testament Scriptures are God-breathed, since their writers spoke from God as they were moved by the Holy Spirit; hence are fully trustworthy in all that they affirm; and are our highest authority for faith and life.

The Church and Its Mission

We recognize the Church as the body of Christ, held together and growing up in him; both as a total fellowship throughout the world, and as the local congregation in which believers gather.

We acknowledge the commission of Christ to proclaim the Good News to all people, making them disciples, and teaching them to obey him.

We acknowledge the command of Christ to love our neighbors, resulting in service to the church and society, in seeking reconciliation for all with God and their fellows, in proclaiming liberty from every kind of oppression; and in spreading Christ's justice in an unjust world … until he comes again.

88

Worldlink's Working Principles

Every year, each member of the Worldlink Board of Directors reviews and affirms their agreement with, and commitment to, Worldlink's Statement of Beliefs and Statement of Working Principles. It is upon these truths and our shared understanding that we join together in shared ministry at Worldlink.

These are our Worldlink Working Principles:

We affirm these basic principles upon which we have built, and continue to build, Worldlink.

1. God wants this generation of believers to bring his tangible love and Good News to this generation of unbelievers worldwide.

2. God has made available to his church all of the resources required to accomplish this task.

3. Indigenous missionaries are uniquely positioned to effectively bring God's love and the Gospel to the people of their countries.

4. Partnerships that equip and empower indigenous missionaries are an effective strategy for spreading the Good News.

5. Christians around the world have been given stewardship of a vast amount of God's resources that he wants to be used to reach the world for Christ.

6. Christians around the world can be motivated to invest God's resources in support of their brothers and sisters on the frontlines of indigenous missionary service.

7. Worldlink can efficiently link God's people and resources with God's servants in the majority world.

8. Worldlink will send 100% of funds designated for indigenous missionaries to the field.

9. God wants Worldlink to continue to grow the number of people reached by continuing to grow the number of indigenous missionaries supported.

10. To grow the number of indigenous missionaries supported we must continually increase the impact of prayer and financial partners.

11. A godly, passionate, capable, and equipped Board and Staff are critical to the success of Worldlink's endeavors.

12. Only with the direction of God and the empowerment of his Spirit will our efforts be fruitful.

Frequently Asked Questions

What is an indigenous missionary?

From a Christian perspective, a missionary is a Christian on a mission to share the love of God and the Good News of Jesus Christ with other people. Some people associate the term "missionary" with a person sharing God's love in another culture or another country. This is not required in the Bible or in today's world.

Worldlink uses the terms indigenous missionary, native missionary, and local missionary to help define our international partners. They are missionaries to the people in the land in which they were born and live.

Where are Worldlink's indigenous missionary partners located?

Simply put, our partners serve in areas with the "Greatest Need and Least Access." Philosophically, our partnerships focus on areas where the local population is unreached or less reached with the Good News. Geographically, this currently includes the following countries:

- **Asia Region:** Bangladesh, Bhutan, India, Indonesia, Myanmar, Nepal, Pakistan, and Sri Lanka

- **Americas Region:** Argentina, Colombia, and Guatemala

- **Africa Region:** Benin, Burkina Faso, Cameroon, Central African Republic, Congo, Democratic Republic of the Congo, Ethiopia, Gambia, Kenya, Lesotho, Liberia, Mozambique,

91

Nigeria, Rwanda, Sierra Leone, South Africa, Swaziland, Tanzania, Togo, Uganda, and Zambia

What advantages do indigenous missionaries have?

Because they are native to the places they serve, there are numerous significant advantages that indigenous missionaries have over a traditional Western missionary.

- Indigenous missionaries are often more effective than their Western counterparts because they have no language, culture, travel, or lifestyle barriers to overcome.

- Indigenous missionaries can live, serve, and travel in closed countries that cannot be reached by Western missionaries.

- Indigenous missionaries do not need to leave the "mission field" for long periods of rest or to raise support back home— since they are already home!

- Indigenous missionaries do not need to abandon the work when regional conflicts arise.

- The work of indigenous missionaries is highly cost-effective. While it costs an average of $40,000 US to $70,000 US a year to support the typical Western missionary, an indigenous missionary can be fully supported for as little as $300 US to $2,000 US a year.

How do you train your missionaries?

Training and equipping of missionaries is based on the very individual needs of the missionary and the context in which they serve. Since we always work with local teams we find that the recommended workers often come with the capacity to do significant ministry in their own context. In most cases though, additional learning can be helpful for ministry effectiveness, so the local teams have the ability to recommend necessary training. Each individual will have differing needs based on the target of their work, but all are required to have basic Bible training.

The level of training is higher for some than for others. For example, a simple village preacher/church planter in India requires much less training to get started than a worker evangelizing college students in an African city.

In addition, we share best practices between regions. For example, what is successful in evangelism in Indonesia might also be applicable to the northern tier of sub-Saharan Africa. We are able to cross-pollinate ideas from around the world.

How do you support your missionaries with supplies?

As with training, supplies are a very individual issue. We generally do not send equipment or materials from the West to our missionary partners. We have found that if supplies are needed they are better if locally procured. This eliminates the problem of "Western" materials being introduced into the context, it helps the indigenous missionary in relationship with vendors from whom they buy supplies, and it thus aids the local economy. So when we want to provide bicycles for native missionary evangelists we do not load a container of bikes and send them over. We send the money to purchase them locally. In this way the relief is immediate, less expensive, and contextually acceptable.

In many of the cultures in which frontline indigenous missionaries serve it is not a benefit to be associated with Western entities. If a native missionary is seen as connected to Western money, ideas, and direction, it tends to produce suspicion of motives and opens the missionary for targeting by maliciously minded opponents.

How do you distribute funds to your missionaries?

We distribute funds to our partners quarterly. Our policy is that 100% of funds that come in designated for our indigenous missionary partners or specific ministries or projects go to that partner/ministry. We raise all funds for operational and administrative support separately.

Each indigenous missionary partner is required to submit their quarterly reports by the first day of the month in which their support is sent. We send the support on the 15th day of the month via wire transfers to our local ministry affiliates. We do not send funds directly to individuals, as we believe that this would undermine local accountability.

How does Worldlink find its indigenous partners?

Through long-standing ministry relationships with indigenous Christian leaders in the developing world, Worldlink has been able to construct reliable webs of relationships which allow us to connect with Christian workers of high character and giftedness for ministry. A thorough process of evaluation, including independent references, is undertaken prior to accepting anyone for partnership.

Many of our relationships began with Jack Nelson, our founder and president, and contacts from his decade of service with Scripture Union, an evangelistic and Bible reading ministry active in over 120 countries. During that time, Jack developed relationships with respected church and ministry leaders in countries around the world. When God led him to start Worldlink, he went to his trusted friends/colleagues to locate people who were ready to be indigenous missionaries in their own countries.

Missionary partners come to us at the recommendation of trusted Christian leaders who can vouch for their character, capability, chemistry, and calling. Then we seek the cash needed to empower them for ministry.

What are Worldlink's partnership criteria?

In seeking to be faithful to the vision and calling set before Worldlink, we also want to be sensitive to the opportunities and needs that God sets before us. To do so requires some structure to categorize and prioritize ministries, programs, and opportunities we see.

We recognize and admit that we are not called to be all things to all people, despite our hearts' desires to serve every opportunity that we encounter. Acknowledging our limited resources, we have developed the following two basic categories for helping us with determining ministry partnerships. When bringing on a partner we look to see if they fit our criteria (do they fit what we think the Lord is leading us to help do) and then our capacity (how many partners do we think that we can help this year and beyond).

The following criteria are the essentials to which any organization/individual must adhere in order to be considered for partnership. All elements must be agreed to and upheld in the course of ministry. These elements have been with Worldlink since inception and are unlikely to change.

- **Christian:** The partnering staff must be followers of Christ and be in agreement with Worldlink's Statement of Beliefs and doctrinal stance. The elements of this statement are consistent with our understanding of Scripture and the historical doctrines of the Christian Church.

- **Evangelistic:** Worldlink's international partners must have as a main emphasis of their efforts the salvation of souls. While we applaud and encourage efforts to share God's love in tangible ways and we employ many efforts that promote pain relief and social/societal change, our unique calling is to expand the Kingdom of God by supporting intentional evangelistic and disciple-making efforts.

- **Indigenously led:** We believe in the ability of Christians who were born and raised in the local context to share the Gospel in faithful, effective, and God-honoring ways that are easily understood by their own culture. Our desire it to encourage and support their efforts, not to direct or control them. We expect that local leadership extends to the board and directors, not just individual staff workers. Though we recognize the value in inviting an external perspective, Worldlink's partners should be making decisions on the ground, free from foreign control.

- **Leveraged:** Worldlink is interested in supporting God's workers doing God's work. However, we do not want to be the sole source of funding for a ministry, and therefore we expect our partnering workers to invite local partners to support their efforts wherever that is possible. This allows greater ownership and commitment by the community and includes them in what God is doing.

- **Areas less-influenced by the Gospel:** This makes sense for both Worldlink's calling and our partner's situations. We are interested in evangelism and discipleship and desire to fulfill Christ's last command to carry his Good News into all the world. Partners serving in areas with little or no Christian presence are in greater need of the financial, material, and spiritual support that Worldlink can offer.

- **A Clear and Demonstrated Calling:** Worldlink is looking for brothers and sisters who believe, with confirmation from respected people who know them, that God is asking them to do the ministry and who are already actively serving while looking to the Lord for provision. Most often they are actively volunteering or serving with minimal support or in a bi-vocational ministry. We are not interested in workers who are looking for a "job"; we are interested in partnering with those who are following a "calling." He or she will have a reputation of being a servant and exhibit a heart of perseverance through whatever hardships might accompany the work.

- **Recommendation:** Worldlink will entertain the possibility of partnership with individuals and/or groups for whom we receive recommendation from our network of trusted friends around the world. We do not entertain self-recommendations.

- **Commendable Character:** Those who work with potential partners should be able to say without hesitation, "This person is of such high Christian character that I have complete confidence that they will do what they say and will honestly report what they did and did not accomplish."

What are Worldlink's partnership preferences?

Our partnerships may change over time based on God's leading, strategic timing, and opportunity. We may prefer a certain geographical region for a number of reasons. We may sense God's leading toward a particular opportunity that may close rapidly. Based upon a variety of factors, partnerships might be one-time, decreasing over time, or ongoing.

Worldlink does not generally partner with established churches in other countries. This is because faithful giving of the

97

local congregation allows for financial support of that local ministry, but, in the areas where we work, local funds are not generally available to missionaries planting churches in unreached areas or operating alongside churches.

Church planters who plan to become pastors will be considered for decreasing financial partnerships. This is based on the understanding that many groups focus evangelistic efforts on creating churches in areas where none exist. Support for these efforts would be required and appropriate. This financial support will be decreased over time as the Gospel takes hold in the community and the church is able to support the work of its minister.

What are the major needs of indigenous missionaries?

For those called to reach their countrymen and women, the needs are wide and varied. Worldlink seeks to provide whatever is needed to overcome barriers to their effective witness. This support may include salary support or supplement; training and sharing of best practices; strategic planning assistance; equipment; pastoral encouragement and support; and prayer support. It's often a lonely road for these faithful servants who are living in areas with little or no Christian presence. It is wonderful for our partners to know that a team from around the world is supporting them in prayer and available to encourage them.

Typically, support includes a small amount of money that is added to locally available support to equal a full-time salary (freeing indigenous missionaries from the daily concern of feeding and sheltering themselves and their families). It also includes helping with additional training. Our networks allow us to connect national Christian workers with opportunities for help with things such as: evangelism in a particular religious or anti-religious context; local fundraising; educational opportunities when opposing forces deny them—especially helping with biblical and doctrinal education; equipment for more effective ministry; and equipment for travel needs.

Why is Worldlink a good option for supporting indigenous missionaries? To whom is Worldlink accountable?

Worldlink is committed to "taking pains to do what is right, not only in the eyes of the Lord but also in the eyes of men" (2 Corinthians 8:21).

Worldlink is led by an independent Board of Directors. The Board Treasurer does an on-site financial review each month. This includes a review of monthly bank reconciliation reports and outgoing missionary support. The treasurer also performs spot audits of income and expense accounts.

Classified by the United States Internal Revenue Service (IRS) as a non-profit 501(c) 3 organization, Worldlink is accountable to both Pennsylvania State and US Federal regulations governing the proper use of donated funds. We are also a member in good standing with the Evangelical Council for Financial Accountability (www.ECFA.org), and we abide by their Seven Standards of Responsible Stewardship (http://www.ecfa.org/Content/7Standards.aspx).

Every year an independent accounting firm audits our financial records. These audits are available for public inspection at our office.

How much does Worldlink withhold from funds donated for international partners?

Nothing. (That is 0%.)

From its inception, Worldlink has been committed to sending 100% of money received for international partners to our international partners. This has been and will continue to be our faithful practice.

Home team staff compensation and operating expenses are raised independent of missionary support.

How are the indigenous missionary partners held accountable?

We agree with an Indian friend who said that accountability is "not a 'Western' thing, not an 'Eastern' thing, but a Jesus thing." Consequently, we expect our partners to regularly inform us about three areas of their life, following the example of the Apostle Paul:

> Tychicus, the dear brother and faithful servant in the Lord, will tell you everything, so that you may know how I am and what I am doing. I am sending him to you for this very purpose, that you may know how we are and that he may encourage you. (Ephesians 6:21-22)

> …they sailed back to Antioch where they had been committed to the grace of God for the work they had now completed. On arriving there, they gathered the church together and reported all that God had done through them and how he had opened the door of faith to the Gentiles. (Acts 14:26-27)

Our international accountability structure includes:

- Quarterly reports based on the topics mentioned above
  - How are the partners and their family doing physically, emotionally, and spiritually?
  - What activities have they done this quarter and what is planned for the next?
  - What results has God brought through the ministry?
- Site visits by area and regional leadership staff

- Site visits by Worldlink US or UK staff
- Review by local contacts
- Significant pre-partnership analysis, prayer, and research (getting the right people and commitments at the start means better relationships down the road).

How does Worldlink address the concern of dependency?

First, we acknowledge that we are all dependent on something or someone. Every right-minded Christian will acknowledge that we are dependent on God. The question is not whether or not we, our native missionary partners, or anyone else, is dependent, but rather "upon whom or what are we dependent?"

Worldlink's international partners, as well as our US and UK staff, look to God rather than to people for sustenance. We are constantly watching our interactions to make sure that we support their ministry goals rather than dictate Western solutions to local concerns.

It is popular to talk about the "three-selfs" in the global church: self-governing, self-propagating, and self-supporting. Worldlink believes that when the first two are true and healthy, the third is not much of an issue.

Dependency can be an unnecessary distraction, or even an excuse, for some Western Christians. We have never heard someone bemoan the fact that a local Western pastor is entirely dependent on the local congregation for their income. We have never heard someone concerned that an inner-city ministry in a poor area of town is funded through a partnership with a suburban church. We have never seen angst in someone over the fact that an outreach ministry in an impoverished rural area is supported through funding from other areas. We have never heard a missions committee express trepidation over "creating dependency" in the lives and ministries of the Western missionaries they are supporting in another part of the world. So, why is it that "creating dependency" is only an issue when we are dealing with people who are different than us? Perhaps the real issue is a trust issue or a control issue.

All funds in the hands of God's people really belong to God. We are not sure that God is awfully concerned whether support for his work comes from a pocket that is 10 feet from the offering plate, 10 miles from the offering plate, or 10 time zones from the offering plate. As long as the minister receiving the funds in support of his or her ministry realizes that all support funds are from the hand of God and it is God, and God alone, upon which the minister is dependent, then which pocket God pulls those funds from is of little consequence.

How can I help Worldlink and its indigenous missionary partners?

First, pray without ceasing. Use the monthly Prayerlink as your guide. You can receive your copy monthly by signing up on the Worldlink website at www.worldlinkonline.org.

Second, be extravagantly generous in your donations. The opportunities that Worldlink's current and prospective indigenous missionary partners have to reach people for Christ far outpace the funds that we currently have to empower them. If you are led, any gifts would be incredibly helpful. Go to the Worldlink website at www.worldlinkonline.org or send in the response card found in this book to support an indigenous missionary. Remember that 100% of funds sent for indigenous missionaries go to that missionary.

Third, become a Worldlink advocate. If you agree with what you've read in this book, tell others of the amazing things God is doing and the amazing ways they can join you and make an immediate and eternal difference in the lives of people in some of the world's hardest places. Free copies of REACHABLE are available by visiting our website.

To schedule Jack Nelson, or someone else from Worldlink, to preach or share with your church or group, contact info@ worldlinkonline.org

What Others Have Said

"Worldlink is a ministry with a mission close to God's heart and a strategy that brings positive results with low expenses and exemplary Christian leadership. I commend Worldlink to you."

—Dr. Philip G. Ryken, President,
Wheaton College, Wheaton, IL

"In my role as Scripture Union International Director, I oversee our work in over 120 countries. In my travels, I have seen first-hand the fruit of Worldlink's native missionary partnerships and the tremendous value and outcomes of their support. I am happy to recommend Worldlink and Jack to you without hesitation."

—Janet Morgan, International Director,
Scripture Union International, London, UK

"As a Christian I am called to reach people around the world with the Gospel. As a business owner I am also called to be a faithful steward of the resources God has blessed me with and to seek to get the highest return on investment of Kingdom resources. Both of these calls are satisfied in the work of Worldlink International Ministries."

—Jeffrey Rose, President, Lifesong for Orphans
Haiti Advocate Board, Delray Beach, FL

"In 2002, when the Lord led Jack to found Worldlink to help spread the Gospel in partnership with native missionaries, I was thrilled because I had experienced first-hand the effectiveness of the native missionaries with whom Jack had connected me.... Without hesitation, I encourage you to join in God's work through Worldlink with your prayers, your investment of time, and your generous financial partnership."

—Rev. Carroll L.G. Wynne, Minister of Pastoral Care, Tenth Presbyterian Church, Philadelphia, PA, and Worldlink Board Member

"Put simply, if Worldlink did not exist, the forward thrust of the Gospel message would be thwarted in many strategic areas. Worldlink has my highest respect and greatest appreciation. Their work is not easy, but it is vital."

—David Jones, Managing Director, Cedarstone, Wheaton, IL

"Worldlink's internal controls and procedures are about as good as any I've seen... Your system is set up very well, and covers all the bases and then some."

—Georgia L.S. Myers, CPA, Director, Canon Capital Certified Public Accountants, Souderton, PA

Now Look What You've Done!

When I was young, the statement, "Now look what you've done!" was exclusively used to draw my attention to the unwanted consequences of some unwise act. It usually involved a hammer, firecrackers, or a model helicopter wheel. Honestly, I was just having fun.

As a teen, that same statement was revisited again in reference to a 1967 military-surplus Plymouth station wagon in a convenience store parking lot. I was not having fun that time. But, those are stories for another book.

I recently dusted off that phrase, repurposed it, and shared it with some of Worldlink's indigenous missionary sponsors. Those dear people became aware of what God was doing through indigenous missionaries (just like you have by reading this book) and were moved to partner with one or more indigenous missionaries whom they will never meet to reach the unreached in a land where they will never visit.

What they had done did not result in bruised fingers, trips to the hospital, or the dented fenders of my youth. No, the small but sacrificial sponsorships had resulted in hundreds of thousands of people hearing the Good News in their own language and culture in a way to which they could respond. And tens of thousands of people responded in faith. And tens of thousands more do so each year.

Their missionary sponsorship resulted in ministry in three areas of emphasis:

- **Outreach.** Often the hearts of spiritually needy people are open to hear of God's grace, so our partners are running evangelistic clubs in Pakistan, Jesus film outreaches in Uganda, Gospel campaigns in Ethiopia, church planting ministries in Indonesia, Bible listening groups in Tanzania, prison visitation in Zambia, Mobile Bible Institute training in India, athletic outreaches in Kenya, and so much more.

- **Mercy.** Often experiencing a touch of God's love is the first step in people's openness to hearing his Good News, so our partners are rescuing victims of war-ignited sexual violence in the Democratic Republic of the Congo, relieving suffering in refugee settlements in Sri Lanka, aiding the persecuted in Nigeria, feeding children in Guatemalan villages, and so much more.

- **Children.** Often the most receptive hearts are the youngest hearts, so our partners are leading Bible camps in Argentina, life skills seminars in Togo, children's homes in India, orphan ministry in Rwanda, ministry to slum children in Colombia, outreaches to former child soldiers in Sierra Leone, school peer Bible clubs in Liberia, Vacation Bible clubs in the Nepal, and so much more.

Section Two of this book is entitled "We Are Worldlink." I invite you to join us. On behalf of thousands of potential indigenous missionaries who await your sponsorship that will unleash them to productive full-time missionary service in their own countries, I urge you to join us. On behalf of billions of people who suffer daily and have never had the chance to understand and respond to God's amazing offer of eternal life, I beg you to join us.

To sponsor an indigenous missionary like the ones you have met in this book, please return the enclosed Response Card, go to www.worldlinkonline.org, or call Worldlink at 610-630-3775. To have interested friends receive a free copy of *Reachable* have them go to www.worldlinkonline.org or call Worldlink at 610-630-3775.

When you join us, we will stand linked together with brothers and sisters across the world, declaring with our voices and proving with our actions that unreached people are REACHABLE.